U[
A Vaping Cautionary Tale
by Kyle Combs

Dedication:

This book is dedicated to the people who have impacted my life in meaningful ways. To my mom and dad, who have always been there for me and supported me through thick and thin. To my late aunt Kathy, who will always hold a special place in my heart. Though she has passed since the writing of this book, I think about her frequently and cherish the memories we shared.

To my uncle Rob, who may get under my skin at times, but I secretly enjoy our bickering. To my brother, who I love dearly, and my nephews, who bring joy and laughter to my life.

I also want to extend my thanks and gratitude to the incredible nurses I met at Kettering Hospital in Kettering, Ohio, who provided me with care and support throughout my journey. To the specialists and doctors who helped me navigate my medical experiences, thank you for your expertise and compassion.

Lastly, I want to express my gratitude to the man who I believe was an angel in disguise. I didn't catch his name, but his words of advice still resonate with me to this day. He seemed to know that I was going through a tough time, and his wisdom and kindness helped me more than he could ever know.

To all these individuals, I dedicate this book to you. Thank you for being a part of my life and for helping me through my experiences.

Preface:

My name is Kyle Combs, and I wrote this book about two years ago. At the time, I didn't know what I was doing, and I lacked the literary knowledge needed to effectively convey my experiences. However, I have since gained more knowledge and experience in writing, and I am confident that this rewritten version will do justice to the story I want to tell.

The original book was titled "Iron-Lung the Worry-Wart," thanks to my mother's input. While I appreciated her suggestion, I have decided to change the title to something else. As I write this preface, I haven't yet decided on a new title. Still, I hope that by the end of the rewrite, I will come up with a title that truly does this story justice.

The events and experiences described in this book are entirely true. I personally experienced them when I was twenty years old, and they still have an effect on me to this day. As a reader, I hope that you can learn something from this book - whether it's to stay away from vaping or simply to face any challenge and overcome it, no matter how much pain and heartache it may cause.

Thank you for reading, and I hope you enjoy the new and improved version of my memoir.

Frozen in Time:

A Memoir of Life in the Cold

With a cart full of raw meat, I pushed my way through the flapping doors. As I entered the refrigerated zone, I couldn't help but feel relieved to be away from the freezing metallic box of the food refrigerator. The bright lights bounced off the brown floor, illuminating my path as I drove my cart up to each vacant unloading point.

This had become my routine for the past 8 hours, ever since I had transitioned to the meat department after finishing high school. At the young age of 19, I was now working full time, grateful for the freedom that came with leaving the front-end.

You see, I had started as a cashier and quickly grew to despise the position due to the cruel behavior of one of the Customer Service Managers. When I applied to transfer, she did everything in her power to keep me upfront, for reasons known only to herself.

But I didn't give up. I suggested coming in for overtime and worked tirelessly to impress my boss and other managers. Eventually, they saw my potential and granted me the transfer, freeing me from the clutches of the benevolent but oppressive CSM.

The CSM I am referring to was truly one of the most obnoxious people I had ever encountered. She seemed to believe that her opinion was of the utmost importance and that she had a right to speak to anyone however she pleased under the guise of being "truthful." She made it her mission to bring others down, and her toxic behavior was difficult to stomach.

Psychologically speaking, individuals like the CSM can be categorized as narcissistic, meaning they possess an inflated sense of self-importance and a deep-seated need for admiration and attention. They often lack empathy and are willing to exploit others for their own gain. It's not uncommon for them to belittle and demean those around them to boost their own egos, while hiding their own insecurities and emotional wounds behind a facade of superiority.

While it was clear that the CSM's life was not a happy one, it was no excuse for her to take out her frustrations on others. Despite her best efforts to keep me at the front-end, I refused to let her defeat me. Through hard work and perseverance, I was able to rise above her toxicity and secure a position in the meat department where I could thrive.

Sadly, the CSM was not the only toxic individual at Walmart. There were many others who shared her toxic traits, making it a challenging environment to work in. It seemed as though some employees had been working there for so long that they had become jaded and unhappy with their lives, taking their frustrations out on their coworkers.

But I refused to let their negativity bring me down. Instead, I focused on my work and tried my best to remain positive. And despite the challenges I faced, I found myself enjoying my time in the meat department. I enjoyed the physical work and the opportunity to interact with customers in a different way than I did when I was a cashier.

In the end, I realized that the toxicity of others could only affect me if I allowed it to. By choosing to rise above it and focus on the positive, I was able to create a better work environment for myself and find fulfillment in my job.

The job in the meat department was a welcome change from the front-end where I had to constantly deal with customers, including rude college kids. I found solace in the freezer, where I could take a break and enjoy a few moments of peace and quiet. The icy chill and the hum of the refrigeration system provided a soothing background, and it was a relief to be away from the chaos and noise of the sales floor. I welcomed the chance to work in an environment where I could focus on my tasks without being interrupted by customers.

My favorite part of the night shift was when the store would slow down and I could indulge in my love for Star Wars and Stephen King books. I had just discovered the Star Wars expanded universe stories, and I was hooked. As a kid, I had seen the movies, but I never really got into the fandom until I stumbled upon these audiobooks. Listening to the stories while surrounded by stacks of meat was an interesting contrast, but it was a welcome escape from the monotony of the job. It was the perfect way to unwind after a long day and keep my mind occupied while I worked. Those moments of escapism helped me get through some tough times at work and in my personal life.

While at work, I formed great relationships with my associates and managers, some of whom had been with the company for over two decades. They had retired from their service, and it felt like I was surrounded by a family of military veterans, which was comforting since my own family had a military background. However, my supervisor was an entirely different story. He turned out to be a snake in the grass, a creep, and a two-faced individual. I later found out about his actions against my other coworkers, and it made me realize that even though I got along with everyone, there was still a dark side to the workplace. Despite forming relationships, I was still lonely, and that loneliness was only compounded by the frigid isolation of the freezer.

Working in the meat department at Walmart had its perks, and one of them was the flexibility of my schedule. I could take my lunch and breaks whenever I wanted, which gave me a sense of freedom that I didn't have before. Another benefit was my pay. I received a substantial pay raise due to my excellent work ethic, which was reflected in my evaluations.

Despite these positives, I still felt a sense of loneliness. Even though I got along with my colleagues and managers, I yearned for deeper connections. However, I found solace in my audiobooks and my love for Star Wars. I had recently discovered the expanded universe stories and had become hooked on them. So during my downtime, I would immerse myself in the world of Jedi knights, Sith lords, and galactic battles. It was a welcome escape from the mundanity of my job and the emptiness I felt inside.

As I worked in the college town of Miami University, I found myself using my charm to catch the attention of female students. It seemed like everything was falling into place for me. I even found myself in a relationship with a co-worker from the front-end named Anjali. She was studying to become a cardiologist, and her intelligence and poise left me questioning why she was interested in a small-town guy like me. Despite our differences, we were committed to each other for a while, proving that the saying "opposites attract" held some truth. Looking back on it now, I realize that Anjali was a beautiful soul who deserved better treatment from me. Unfortunately, our relationship eventually fell apart.

My ultimate goal was to become the department manager for the frozen food section, a position held by the brother of a former friend who used to babysit me. He was moving on to bigger and better things, so I worked tirelessly to become the next in line. I took all the required tests, including the online video tests, and even received valuable guidance from the current manager on how to use the computer software to order and manage inventory. I was determined to learn all the ins and outs of the handheld devices we used, and my confidence was unwavering. I was passionate about this position and pursued it with all my heart. Looking back now, I realize that I am more than qualified for the job, and if I were to return to that Walmart, they would practically offer me the position on a silver platter.

My typical day at work consisted of me heading to the refrigerator to discard the crates left over from the previous shift, followed by moving to the meat wall to scan and refill empty spaces using my scanner. This was a repetitive cycle that I carried out for 8 hours straight, with occasional trips to the back to retrieve packed food, all while hoping to avoid getting splattered with blood. The freezer was my go-to spot for most of the day, and the constant smell of rotting meat, which was meant to be shipped out to dog food factories, was an added unpleasant experience that I had to endure.

As I reminisce about my time at the store, one particular memory still sends shivers down my spine - entering the dreaded seafood freezer. The moment I stepped inside, I was greeted by a frigid blast of air that could turn even the warmest blood to ice. The temperature was so low that a layer of ice had formed on the floor, making each step treacherous. As I reached for the metal shelves, my fingers would instantly stick to the surface, leaving behind patches of torn skin. Oh, how I despised that freezer and the bone-chilling horrors it held.

After a month had passed, November had arrived, and I began to notice something peculiar. As I took a puff of my vape (yes, I was one of those people), I struggled to inhale a sufficient amount of vapor. The clouds that I produced were not as impressive as I had initially thought they would be, and were similar to those of any other regular smoker. Unfortunately, my breathing problems were not just limited to vaping. I had been smoking cigars, hookahs, cigarettes, and pipes as well, and I was finding it increasingly difficult to breathe. It's worth noting that I frequented the hookah lounge in Oxford from time to time as well.
As I traveled longer distances, I began to realize that I needed to catch my breath more often. Initially, I thought it was just a chest cold, and since I smoked, I didn't want to be overly concerned. I didn't want to worry unnecessarily, so I ignored it and hoped it would improve with time. However, a mild pain began to grow on the left side of my chest, and I also started to develop a deep, raspy cough.

As my health deteriorated, I began to realize the gravity of my smoking habit. My girlfriend Anjali was getting increasingly upset with me, constantly urging me to quit. She even went as far as to tell me that she wouldn't be there if I ever ended up in the hospital with lung cancer. As harsh as those words were, I knew she said them out of love and concern for my well-being. She was always such an honest person.

As I lay down to rest, I couldn't help but feel this strange, bubbling sensation in my lungs, every breath I took sounding like a gurgling swamp. It was disconcerting, to say the least. Gradually, it became increasingly difficult to draw in air, and being the worrier I am, I booked an appointment with my family doctor.

Regrettably, my regular family doctor was on vacation, and so I had to visit his son, who also practices medicine. As a habitual smoker with an innate fear of medical professionals and facilities, I smoked my way to the doctor's office to address my breathing issues. Irony at its finest. Upon explaining my symptoms, one of the doctor's first orders of business was to advise me to quit smoking.

At the doctor's office, it seemed pretty clear that smoking was the culprit behind my breathing issues. He handed me a prescription for an inhaler, Ventolin, and I left feeling more determined than ever to kick my smoking habit to the curb. And so, as soon as I arrived home, I started throwing away all of my smoking tools. The pipe, the hookah, the cigars, and the cigarettes - all of it had to go. But the toughest one to part with was my beloved vape. I had spent a small fortune on mods and juice, and the thought of giving it up was painful. However, I knew it had to be done, so I sold it off for half the price and said goodbye to my cloudy companions.

At work, my determination to become a better version of myself was at an all-time high. Not only was I excelling in my role, but I also started reading self-help books like "How to Make Friends and Influence People" to improve my confidence. I knew I had always struggled with self-assurance, often finding myself becoming a recluse and closing myself off from the world. But now, I was determined to change that. Although I still considered myself a self-proclaimed recluse, I was becoming more socially adept with each passing day.

In the weeks that followed, I started to notice some improvements at work. My persistent wet cough, which previously yielded no results, began to loosen up, allowing me to breathe a little more comfortably. And since I refrained from smoking during my breaks, my condition wasn't aggravated. However, the inhaler that my doctor prescribed me had a peculiar side-effect - it made me cough up phlegm, which was quite repulsive, I admit. But unfortunately, as you'll soon find out, things were about to take a turn for the worse.

The coughing fits were relentless and grew increasingly violent, leaving me feeling utterly drained. It was perplexing because it had been more than a week since my last smoke, yet my lungs still felt like they were on fire. Each time I inhaled the frigid air, it felt like tiny needles were piercing through my chest, triggering another bout of coughing. Driving home was even more challenging; the heat from the vents would blast onto my face, making me gasp for air. It was a lose-lose situation, with no respite in sight.

Every night when I would come home from work, I'd trudge up the stairs to my room and by the time I reached the top, I'd be gasping for air. It was as if the stairs had turned into a daunting mountain that I had to conquer just to reach my own bed. Desperate to catch my breath, I'd fumble for my inhaler and take a puff of Ventolin. The taste was like a combination of mint and rust, a metallic tang that filled my mouth and nose. But, as strange as it may sound, that taste was oddly comforting, because it meant that relief was on its way. The pain that had been growing in my chest, a constant nagging presence, would finally subside and I could breathe normally again.

As time went on, the coughing fits became even more intense, to the point where I was hacking up thick liquid from my lungs. Initially, I attributed it to the e-liquid residue from my vape that might have found its way into my lungs. But the amount of fluid that I was coughing up soon became excessive. It was as if I had accidentally inhaled a substantial amount of water while swimming and was trying to cough it all out, but three times worse. The sensation was unpleasant and left me feeling drained and exhausted.

As I lounged in my armchair, engrossed in the TV show, an intense heat erupted in the middle of my back. It felt like a fiery spear was piercing through my skin, scorching every nerve ending in its path. The pain was unbearable, and I couldn't help but break out in a cold sweat. The nausea hit me like a freight train, and I stumbled to the bathroom in a daze. Straining to relieve myself, I soon realized that it was impossible. In desperation, I grabbed some muscle cream, hoping it would dull the agony, but it only offered temporary relief. For a whole hour, I endured the excruciating pain until, as suddenly as it had appeared, it vanished into thin air.

As the winter settled in, I found myself going through the motions of my job, scanning the empty spaces on the food racks, and bantering with my supervisor. The back pain that had been plaguing me for weeks was now a constant companion, but I tried to ignore it as best as I could. I popped Ibuprofen like candy, hoping it would provide some relief. As we prepared the food donations, we laughed and joked, trying to make the mundane task a little more bearable. But as soon as it was over, I retreated back to my solitary existence. The frigid air stung my face, and I began to cough uncontrollably. I fumbled for my inhaler and a paper towel, which had become my constant companions. Every day, I made sure to have a handful of paper towels within arm's reach. As I pressed the inhaler to my mouth, I noticed something amiss. A few droplets of blood stained the paper towel.

The liquid on the paper towel was unmistakably red, thin and runny - it was definitely blood. The taste of metal lingered in my mouth, confirming my worst fears. Panic rose inside me like a tidal wave, and my mind raced through every possible scenario, all of them ending with the same dreaded word: cancer.

I stood frozen in place for what felt like an eternity, my mind grappling with the terrifying realization of what had just happened. It was like a surreal nightmare that I couldn't wake up from. Eventually, my thoughts turned to the practicalities of the situation. I couldn't risk contaminating the food, and I couldn't continue working with this heavy burden weighing on my mind.

As I struggled to process the situation, I found myself overwhelmed by fear and uncertainty. The thought of facing something so terrifying had paralyzed me, leaving me unable to take action or make decisions. All I could do was stand there, staring at the paper towel in my hand, as the world around me continued to spin out of control.

As I stumbled towards the bathroom, my hands shaking with a mix of fear and uncertainty, I couldn't help but feel a sense of dread creeping over me. The metallic taste of blood still lingered in my mouth, and my mind was racing with worst-case scenarios. As I made my way through the swing doors and into the back of the store, I felt a pit forming in my stomach. I approached my manager, feeling like I was in a daze, and managed to mumble that I wasn't feeling well before clocking out.

The drive home was a blur, the streetlights blurring together as my mind raced. I felt like I was in a nightmare that I couldn't wake up from. As I finally pulled into my driveway, I couldn't help but ask myself, "Why me?". I stumbled through the front door and went straight to bed, the fear and uncertainty still palpable in the air around me.

I jolted awake the next morning, my mind racing with anxiety as I knew I had to call off work and schedule a doctor's appointment. The phone seemed to taunt me as it rang and rang until finally, a receptionist answered.
"Hello, Doctor Thompson's office, how can I help you today?"
My heart pounded as I replied, "Yeah, I'd like to set up an appointment, today preferably."
The receptionist shuffled papers on her desk before replying, "Okay, well, I'll set you up for 1:30."
I exhaled a sigh of relief, "Okay. Thank you, goodbye," and hung up the phone.

I dragged myself out of bed, my mind racing with fear and uncertainty. As I stumbled downstairs, the weight of my thoughts only grew heavier. I made my way into the bathroom and turned on the shower, hoping the hot water would wash away my anxiety along with the grime of the previous day.

But my thoughts were unrelenting, playing out worst-case scenarios in my head. "It can't be anything else but cancer," I muttered to myself. "The blood, the sickness... it's all there."

As I lathered myself with soap, my mind somehow drifted to the TV show Breaking Bad. It was about a high school chemistry teacher who turns to cooking and selling crystal meth after being diagnosed with lung cancer. The parallel between my situation and the show's main character was eerie, to say the least.

I shook my head, trying to rid myself of the thought. Lung cancer was a serious matter, and I didn't need to be reminded of it by a TV show.
The thought shook me to my core. I did what any rational person would do, right? The night before, I scoured every Google search result for my symptoms. It wasn't the wisest choice, but I was scared. Every search result pointed to two terrifying possibilities: cancer and pneumonia.

Now, the reason why cancer immediately crossed my mind is because of my family history. Both of my grandparents on my mom's side passed away from various forms of cancer. My grandfather had brain cancer, and my grandmother had colon cancer. Unfortunately, she passed away before I was born, but I still remember vividly my grandfather's death in an Indianapolis hospital when I was only 5 or 6 years old. The sound of his flatline still echoes in my mind, and it's certainly not an experience a child should witness. To this day, it's shaped my perspective on death and related matters.

Years before this, I had a scare when they suspected I had colon cancer in my youth. It all began when I noticed blood in my stool. It seemed like a recurring theme with my health issues, always starting with blood. I had to go through several tests and procedures at the time, which left a lasting impression on me. The fear of contamination gripped my body and soul. It wasn't until 2020 that I was finally diagnosed with ulcerative colitis after years of misdiagnosis with irritable bowel syndrome.

The prospect of undergoing painful cancer tests was not foreign to me, as I had witnessed the grueling process with my aunt. She had been battling cancer for nine years before passing away, leaving a void in our family that is still felt to this day. The diagnosis had taken a toll on her and our entire family, and I knew all too well the devastating effects it can have. Despite this, my uncle has found happiness again and remarried a wonderful woman, but the loss of my aunt still weighs heavily on my heart.

As I walked into the doctor's office, memories of my last visit came rushing back. Last time, I saw the doctor's son, and this time I hoped to see the real deal. I remember wearing this hideous maroon jacket that I snagged for a measly twenty bucks at Walmart, paired with a matching maroon beanie that gave off a sort of turban vibe, and topped it off with some comfy sweatpants. Little did I know that this outfit would be a symbol of things to come.

As I sat in the waiting room, time seemed to drag on forever. The walls were a pale shade of blue and the lighting was fluorescent, making the whole room feel sterile and cold. Finally, the nurse called my name and I walked back to the exam room. She weighed me and my heart dropped as I saw that I had lost 15 pounds. That might not seem like much, but when you're normally 155 pounds, it's a significant amount.

I knew I had to brace myself for what was to come. The thought of grueling tests and painful procedures made my stomach turn. But I also knew that I needed to face this head-on. My mind was racing with all sorts of scenarios, but deep down, I knew that I was ready to handle whatever the doctor would say.

As the doctor, whom I affectionately call "Doc" in real life, enters the room, I can't help but feel a sense of unease wash over me. He takes one look at me and notes, "Looks like you've dropped a few pounds." I force a chuckle in response, trying to ease the tension in the room.

One of my quirks is that when faced with nerve-wracking situations, I tend to laugh or try to find humor in them. Despite my best efforts to control it, my chest was throbbing with pain as I sat in front of the doctor. I mustered up the courage to speak and explained that I had visited the clinic a month prior with a similar issue, but instead of improving, it had only worsened.

As I sat nervously in front of my doctor, I couldn't help but feel a little embarrassed as I pulled out the stained towel from my bag. But desperate times call for desperate measures, and I wanted to make sure he saw the severity of the situation firsthand. His eyes furrowed as he examined the towel, taking note of the amount of blood. I could tell he was concerned, and so was I.

I quickly launched into my explanation, detailing how I had come to him a month prior with the same issue, hoping it would go away on its own. But it only got worse with time. Despite my efforts to quit smoking, it didn't seem to help. I had hoped it was just pneumonia, given that I worked in a freezer for a living and it was winter time. But deep down, I knew it was something more serious.

With a swift motion, he reached for a sleek thermometer and aimed it towards my forehead. It was one of those modern ones that scan your temperature without even touching you. As he finished, he reached for his stethoscope and placed it on my chest. I could feel my labored breathing as he listened closely to my lungs, trying to uncover the source of my discomfort.

"Your temperature is 101.0 degrees, indicating a fever," the doctor said, his tone serious. "We need to take a look inside your chest to figure out what's going on in there. Head across the hallway and get an X-ray done, so we can get a better idea of what we're dealing with."

As I entered the X-ray room, I felt a sense of unease. The bright white lights and sterile smell made it feel more like a lab than a medical facility. The technician directed me to stand in front of a large board, which reminded me of those police line-up scenes from movies. The X-ray machine whirred and hummed as it captured images of my chest. Snap, turn, snap. The process was quick, but the wait for the doctor felt like an eternity.

As I sat there, coughing up fluid and feeling like a prisoner in a bomb shelter, I couldn't help but notice the nurses sitting behind a thick protective barrier. It looked like something out of a sci-fi movie, as if they were guarding against a potential radioactive outbreak. I couldn't help but wonder what they knew that I didn't.

As Doc entered the room, I felt a knot in my stomach, wondering what the x-ray would reveal. He pulled the picture out and my eyes immediately locked onto the large clouding in the underside of my left lung. It looked like a storm brewing inside my chest. The white patches dominated a large portion of the image, making me feel like I was staring at an alien landscape.

Doc's concerned expression only confirmed my fears. "Oh, that doesn't look good at all," he said, his voice heavy with worry. He turned to face me and asked, "How are you feeling? Really."

I felt a lump form in my throat and struggled to speak. "I mean, I haven't been feeling good," I managed to choke out. "I just assumed I had a cold or something because I work in the freezers at Walmart."

He didn't seem convinced. "Well, judging by this picture, you should be in the hospital! How are you even walking around? I mean, you don't look like you're in pain."

Meanwhile, the nurses stationed behind their protective barrier looked on with concern, as if they were witnessing a ticking time bomb.

My heart dropped to my feet, my mind racing with worst-case scenarios. "Is it...is it cancer?" I asked, my voice barely above a whisper. The doctor frowned in response, studying the X-ray once more before shaking his head. "No, I don't think so. If anything, it's a severe case of pneumonia or bronchitis at best," he replied. He jotted down an address and phone number on a slip of paper, handing it to me. "I'm gonna refer you to a specialist. You need to get this looked at right away."

The appointment came to a close, and I left the doctor's office feeling numb. I knew I had to take the week off, and luckily, I had gotten FMLA to help me manage my ongoing health battle.

As soon as I arrived home and shared the news with my parents, they bombarded me with questions. Did I fall? How's my breathing? Is it serious? I tried my best to answer them all. But before my appointment with the specialist, I took it upon myself to do some research and draw my own conclusions.

At 19 years old, freshly out of high school, I had never gone to a doctor's appointment without my parents. But this time, I was on my own, and I knew I had to muster up some courage. As I dialed the number to the specialist's office, a nurse answered, and I quickly provided her with my name and information.

As I spoke to the nurse over the phone, she instructed me to bring in the x-rays from my previous doctor's office. I found it odd that they didn't have access to the records, and as it turned out, I was right to be skeptical. I rushed to my family doctor's office, only to find out that their printer was out of order. Frustrated, I resorted to taking a picture of the x-ray using my phone. Despite this setback, I continued on my journey to see the specialist in Hamilton, OH - a daunting hour-long trip. Looking back, I remember feeling hesitant to name the original doctor and his inadequate services in my initial account back in 2019, but now, I don't care - I am calling him out for his shortcomings.

As I entered the waiting room, the air was thick with the sounds of coughing and wheezing from the elderly patients around me. I felt like a fish out of water, being the youngest person there, separated from the nurse. Eventually, they called my name and led me to a small room where I had to perform breathing exercises. The nurse's concerned expression didn't bode well. Finally, the infamous Dr. Richard S walked in, took a seat, and opened his laptop.

As I began to explain my medical issue, Dr. Richard S interrupted me mid-sentence with a sharp, impatient tone. "What are you in here for?" he demanded. I explained about the fluid around my left lung, but when he asked if I brought in the x-ray, I had to admit I only had a picture of it on my phone. His response was a disgusted, "Well, that doesn't help a whole lot." His condescending attitude was a shock, especially since I was a new patient seeking help for a serious issue. It was clear he thought I was responsible for his inability to access the x-ray properly.

It was frustrating to realize that Dr. S was not only rude but also seemed to lack basic knowledge about how medical records and networks functioned. All of the medical facilities I had visited were under the Tri-Health network, which meant that my files should have been easily accessible to him. Yet, he was blaming me for not bringing in the x-ray and even seemed annoyed when I told him I had taken a picture of it with my phone.

It was clear that Dr. S was not someone who cared about his patients or their well-being. I couldn't help but feel angry and disappointed at the lack of professionalism and empathy shown by this supposed medical professional.

"I apologize, but as I mentioned earlier, the printer was out of order," I replied in a calm tone.
He gave a condescending smirk and said, "It's okay, I'll just have to run an ultrasound on it," as if he was blaming me for the inconvenience.
I couldn't help but match his tone as I replied, "Got it, dude," adding a hint of disdain in my voice.

I had to remove my shirt as Doctor S prepared to perform the ultrasound. The chilly sensation of the cool gel and crisp air made me shiver. After that, he grabbed his stethoscope and tapped it against my ribs while closely monitoring my breathing.

As the doctor stopped the examination and walked over to his computer, I could feel my heart pounding in my chest. When he turned back to me and spoke, his words hit me like a ton of bricks. "Well, I'll explain to you," he said, "it's what they call a pleural effusion. It's most frequent in the elderly, who have pneumonia. That's why it's a little unsettling that you even have this issue because you look fine. But judging by the extent, it unnerves me. Sometimes when individuals get this measure, there's a trace of malignancy (Cancer)." I was stunned, and my mouth felt dry as cotton. My palms went numbly cold as I tried to process what he had just told me.

For context, a pleural effusion is a medical condition where there is an abnormal accumulation of fluid in the pleural cavity, which is the space between the lungs and the chest wall. The pleural cavity normally contains a small amount of fluid to help lubricate the lungs as they expand and contract during breathing. However, in a pleural effusion, there is an excessive buildup of fluid that can cause pressure on the lungs, making it difficult to breathe. Pleural effusions can be caused by a variety of conditions, including infections, heart failure, liver or kidney disease, cancer, or trauma.
"Understood," I replied, trying to hide the panic rising in my chest. "Next week, I'll come to the hospital in Hamilton, OH," he continued, "and we'll perform a thoracentesis. It's a procedure where we'll insert a needle between your ribs to drain out some of the fluid for testing. It's important to get that fluid out to avoid complications in the future. I must warn you, though, this procedure may cause your lung to collapse. But don't worry, I've only had that happen twice before," he explained, almost nonchalantly. It is worth mentioning that the doctor's bedside manner was quite poor, which can make a patient feel uncomfortable and anxious during an already stressful situation.

To provide more context, a thoracentesis is a medical procedure where a needle or small tube is inserted through the chest wall into the pleural space to remove excess fluid or air. This is typically done under local anesthesia and with imaging guidance to ensure safety and accuracy. The removed fluid or air can then be tested to determine the cause of the effusion and guide further treatment.

As for pleural effusions, if left untreated, the fluid can become thicker and more viscous, leading to a condition called a "loculated" effusion, where the fluid is trapped in small pockets and difficult to remove. In some cases, the fluid can also become infected, leading to a serious condition called empyema.

It is important to note that while a thoracentesis can be a safe and effective procedure, there are potential risks and complications that must be carefully considered and discussed with your healthcare provider.

After the appointment was finally over, I made the long and difficult journey back home. The doctor's terrible bedside manner had left me feeling angry and upset, and the news of my condition only made it worse. I tried to distract myself by turning up the radio as loud as possible, but I was still so overwhelmed that my back ached and my stomach churned. Eventually, I had to pull over and vomit. The entire interaction with the doctor kept playing over and over in my mind, haunting me with each passing moment.

The what-if's and what-could-have-beens were racing through my mind. The anger and hostility towards the doctor were still palpable. Despite it all, I attempted to return to work that week. My boss had me stationed outside the refrigerator, just to keep me away from the cold. I aimlessly wandered around the area until the clock struck eleven, and then I just went home. What was the point of being at work if I couldn't technically work? While most people might have enjoyed the break, I despised it. I needed to work and keep myself active. After all, I was saving up money to return to school as an Information Technology Support Major. By this time, me and Anjali had also broken up.

As much as I wanted to pursue my dream of going back to school as an Information Technology Support Major, the mounting medical bills were draining my finances. I confided in my parents about my worries, but they simply advised me to trust in God and pray. It's easier said than done when you're grappling with your own fears and struggles. It seemed like I had hit rock bottom, but life had other plans to knock me down even further. It was exhausting and there were countless nights when even sleep couldn't provide solace. During this time, my faith in the Christian God began to falter, and I started to resent the idea of a higher power. It would be years later before I found my way back to Him.

I would spend the entire night tossing and turning, consumed by worry and endless thoughts. The pain in my back was so intense that

I would often make the mistake of turning to Google for answers, only to find that it caused more harm than good.

In hindsight, it's now 2023 and reflecting back on the events that occurred, I realize that at the time I had everything going for me. I had a job that I loved and a supportive family and group of friends. However, my situation was complicated by my insatiable desire for marijuana. My habit started in high school, during my senior year, and when I couldn't afford real weed, I turned to CBD products. I would go to Wild Berry in Oxford, Ohio, or my local gas station and buy CBD syrup, which costed $15 a bottle. I would mix it with Sprite to create a sort of lean and get high off it. While some argue that you can't get high on CBD, in large amounts, you certainly can. This need to get high would later lead to even worse consequences in my story.

Unveiling the Unwelcome: Facing the Harsh Truth of my Thoracentesis Results

On Monday, my mom accompanied me to the hospital, and I felt relieved to have her support. I didn't care about wearing my big boy pants, as my priority was getting through the procedure. We arrived at Hamilton, OH, and the room we were directed to was square-shaped with a blueish-teal curtain that covered the entrance. I noticed a small flat-screen TV in the corner and immediately switched it on. We settled on watching one of my all-time favorite movies, Planes, Trains, and Automobiles. I have a soft spot for comedies, especially those featuring John Candy or Chris Farley, as they remind me of my dad, and we would always watch them together.

By that time, my fears had subsided and I was finally able to relax. The doctor eventually arrived and his first question was whether I had brought the x-rays. Unfortunately, I had completely forgotten about them. Thankfully, the doctor was able to use the ultrasound again to locate the area of concern. It's worth noting that it's not always the patient's responsibility to provide the doctor with medical records, as hospitals have their own systems in place.

I was instructed to sit on the hospital bed and rest my arms on a small stand. The doctor inserted a needle into my back and it quickly became numb. As the doctor inserted the larger needle, I could feel it moving inside me, a sensation that was completely foreign to me. He then attached a cylinder needle and began to extract fluid from my body, draining it into a large bottle. It felt like I was being transformed into a living oil rig.

My heart began to race, and my breaths became more labored. With each passing moment, I could feel my lung slowly expanding, and soon, I began to cough uncontrollably. My mother held onto my hand tightly as I felt a tingling sensation spread across my face, causing me to fling my glasses across the room. Cold sweat started to trickle down my forehead, and I couldn't stop groaning, coughing, and gasping for air. The pain was excruciating, and my vision began to blur. I knew that if it persisted any longer, I would faint.

The doctor's words hit me hard as he said, "That's not good. This is looking awfully bloody. Normally this stuff is yellow, but this is just straight red. I have a suitable amount, I am gonna quit now." He abruptly stopped and began removing everything from my back before bandaging it up. I watched in silence as he gathered his things and walked out of the room, followed by the nurse carrying my fluid.

As I sat there with my mom, we both were taken aback by the amount and color of the fluid that was drained from me. The doctor had removed a liter of fluid, which had a strikingly similar color to that of cranberry. My mom was visibly shaken by this discovery.

After about 10 minutes, my mom asked, "Well, what's going on? Did Dr. S leave?"

"They might have to send that stuff to the lab," I replied.

"No, I get that. But are you free to leave or what? Did he tell you if you had anything else to do?"

I shook my head.

We sat there for another 10 minutes when I finally had enough, so I paged a nurse. She walked in and asked if I needed anything and I said, "Yeah, I would like to know if I'm good to go or not?"

"I don't know, what are you in here for?" she asked.

"I'm here with Dr. S, he had to do a thoracentesis on me. Is he gonna come back or what's the story here?"

"Oh, Dr. S already left. I'll go see if they want you to do anything else today."

So once again, we waited. After another 10 minutes, she came back in and said, "Well, it looks like he wants to do a CT scan on you today, so let me get this IV in your arm."

This lackluster treatment from Dr. S was becoming a recurring theme. Each time I visited him, I felt like just another patient, another number to check off his list. There was no warmth or empathy in his manner, just a cold and detached professionalism that left me feeling uneasy and unimportant.

As the nurse poked on top of my hand, I stood up and followed her to the radiology department. Dr. S's lackluster treatment was becoming all too familiar. When we arrived at the CT scan room, everything was already set up and ready to go. The machine was a large cylinder that made a loud noise when it started spinning. I lay down on the bed and the nurse placed a pillow under my head and butt.

Since I had stomach issues the year before, I was no stranger to CT scans. As the nurse hooked up the fluid to my IV, she warned me, "When we're ready to take the picture, you're going to taste something nasty in the back of your throat. That's the contrast material going through your IV. Don't worry, and it might make your bottom feel a little warm."

I chuckled and replied, "Yes, ma'am."

As the bed inched forward, the CT scan machine roared to life, emitting a loud whooshing sound that made my heart race. Behind the protective blast shield, the nurse instructed me to put my arms behind my head, warning that I would soon experience a disagreeable taste in my mouth.

"Okay. Now hold your breath," instructed the nurse. As the fluid entered my bloodstream, a warm sensation gradually spread from my stomach to my legs, making me feel like I had just soiled myself. Panicking, I thought, "Oh no, I just crapped my pants."
"You can breathe now," said the nurse, putting an end to my panic. The warmth subsided, and I realized that my fear was unfounded.

The bed slid back, and the nurse removed the fluid tube and my IV. When the other nurse returned, she informed me that I was free to go and advised me to contact the doctor.

At this point, my respect for Dr. S had diminished a bit. However, I still decided to call him because all I wanted was to get better. He scheduled me to come back on Thursday of that week.

The night before my appointment, I was fast asleep in my room when I suddenly woke up to my heart racing, pounding against my chest so hard that I could hear each individual pulse. My face began to feel extremely hot. I sat up, but it seemed to make my heart beat even faster. I thought to myself, "Am I having a heart attack?"

My heart was racing faster than a cheetah chasing its prey. I bolted out of bed and rushed into my parent's room, panting heavily. My dad was sound asleep, but I had no time to waste. "Dad, we need to go to the hospital! I think I'm having a heart attack!" I exclaimed.

My dad tried to calm me down, but my heart was pounding so hard that it felt like it was about to burst out of my chest. We braved the freezing night and made it to the hospital, but the ride felt like an eternity. I could feel my pulse in my throat, and it seemed like every second was taking an eternity.

When we finally arrived, the medical staff rushed me to the EKG machine, a heart monitor that would determine whether or not I was having a heart attack. My nerves were shot, and I could barely keep my composure. After the test, the doctor ordered an X-ray, which thankfully came back negative for a heart attack. It was already three in the morning by the time we left the hospital, and I was exhausted and frightened.

A few days later, we visited Dr S who suggested a bronchoscopy, a procedure that involves a small camera being inserted through the nose and into the lungs to check for any tumors or other issues. The results weren't back yet, but it was a terrifying thought that there could be something growing inside of me.

As I sat in the waiting room with my dad, who had made a joke about being hungry, the atmosphere was tense. Dr. S entered the room with a stern expression on his face and shot my dad a disapproving look. Confused, I asked the doctor what was wrong. He remained silent, and I couldn't help but feel frustrated with his lack of communication. At this point, I was starting to lose faith in him as a doctor, as he seemed more like a fly-by-night practitioner.

As I lay there in agony, my faith wavered, and I felt like I had been abandoned. I looked up to the heavens and cried out to God, my voice shaking with anger and despair. "Why me?" I asked. "What did I do to deserve this?" I had always believed that God was fair, that He rewarded the good and punished the bad. But now, as I lay there in pain, my beliefs were being shattered. I begged Him to end my suffering, making promises and clinging to the hope that things would get better. But as time passed, it felt like God was mocking me, as if my pain was a cruel joke. The doubts crept in, and I struggled to make sense of it all. The questions and the pain were slowly breaking me down.

Despite the upcoming bronchoscopy, my family and I decided to take a weekend trip to Gatlinburg, Tennessee during Christmas Parade season to spend some quality time together. It was a much-needed break from the stress and anxiety of my medical situation, and I even rented a scooter to cruise around on. To my surprise, I ended up on the news not as an interviewee, but as the person zipping around in the background on my scooter. Despite the looming uncertainty of my health, I tried to make the most of our weekend getaway and have some fun. After a memorable weekend, we returned home to prepare for the bronchoscopy.

As we pulled up to Fort Hamilton in Hamilton, Ohio for the surgery, my nerves were on edge. However, the sight of a massive Christmas tree made entirely of twinkling lights with the sweet sounds of holiday music eased my anxiety. As we made our way inside, I couldn't help but feel uneasy about what they might find during the procedure. The nurses began prepping me for surgery, starting with the IV and saline to hydrate me. I found myself in a hospital gown with my backside exposed, but thankfully a warm blanket was draped across my body. Suddenly, the anesthesiologist appeared and began asking me about my medication and any allergies I may have.

As I waited for my surgery, my mind drifted back to the weekend before. But my thoughts were interrupted by the sound of a little old woman next to me talking to a doctor about her recent lung cancer diagnosis. My heart went out to her, and I couldn't help but wonder if I would be next. However, my musings were cut short when, 15 minutes later, they called me back for my own procedure.

Entering the surgical room can be overwhelming for someone who has never experienced it before. But for me, I knew the drill. Nurses and surgeons were bustling around, preparing for my surgery under the blinding light of a big, round fluorescent bulb overhead. As they lifted me onto the operating table, I couldn't help but worry about the IV they had just placed. Luckily, a friendly nurse from my home state of Indiana struck up a conversation with me to pass the time.

Then, the surgeon entered the room and asked if I understood the procedure they were about to perform. Reciting the information I had gathered from both the doctor and the internet, I nodded my understanding.

To ensure that you understand the procedure and the associated risks, they confirm your comprehension before proceeding. Next, they administered an anesthetic into my IV that caused paralysis, and a nurse placed a mask over my face. Darkness followed.
When I woke up, I was back in my room, feeling tired and alone since my parents went to eat. My throat felt scratchy, so I pressed the call button, and a nurse came to give me water and ice. I couldn't help but worry and think. When my parents returned, I felt a lot better. However, my throat still hurt, and I started coughing, and blood came out. We called the nurse in, and she said it was normal because they not only take pictures of the inside of your lungs but also cut out a small piece of tissue to be tested.
Unfortunately, that night my chest hurt, and my heart pounded, and I had to return to the hospital. Despite being connected to an EKG, they found nothing wrong. They did another CT scan and X-ray, and they concluded that it was a panic attack. These attacks became more

common as time went on. Instead of going to the hospital every night, I went to my family doctor, and they prescribed Xanax.

Xanax is a medication that belongs to a class of drugs called benzodiazepines. It works by enhancing the effects of a neurotransmitter in the brain called gamma-aminobutyric acid (GABA), which helps to calm down the activity of certain nerve cells in the brain. Xanax is commonly prescribed to treat anxiety and panic disorders, as well as other conditions such as insomnia and seizures.

However, Xanax has a high potential for abuse and dependence. When taken in large amounts or for long periods of time, Xanax can lead to addiction, withdrawal symptoms, and even overdose. It can also cause a range of side effects, such as drowsiness, dizziness, confusion, and impaired coordination.

With all these in mind, this is where I first was introduced to these kinds of pills. Before this I was totally against pills like this. But when I was prescribed Xanax I was in love, I could finally get the sleep I needed adn it calmed me down. Showing first signs of my addictive personality.

I believed that taking Xanax was my only option, even though I dislike taking drugs that have the potential to become a gateway to addiction. I had experienced this before with Percocet after my hernia surgery a few months earlier. I became addicted and continued taking them to alleviate the withdrawal symptoms. This is why I avoid taking anything that is potentially addictive, as I have a tendency towards addictive behavior. This is evident from my past experience with tobacco, as I had tried every type of tobacco product available to me.

The doctor contacted me with the results, which showed no signs of malignancy, but they still couldn't determine the cause of the pleurisy in my lung. The uncertainty left me feeling uneasy, and I was scheduled to return in a few weeks to discuss removing the remaining fluid. I had to take a month off work to deal with everything. While the news was good, my anxiety and fears continued to consume me. I struggled to keep my emotions in check, and eventually, I became mentally exhausted. I spent most of my time sleeping, either due to my sickness or just to escape my thoughts. On top of everything, my relationship with Anjalil was completely ended when she transferred to Columbus. I fell into a deep depression, feeling like I was drowning in my own life.

After taking Xanax, I began to recover and feel better. The medication helped me to relax and ease my worries. Even though I was still unable to work, I managed to visit my colleagues and travel a bit. However, it was disheartening that I had nobody to rely on except my parents. None of my friends checked in on me, and people who used to talk to me regularly seemed to vanish into thin air. Even the kids I grew up with and went to school with, nobody was there. It's worth mentioning that now, four years later, I completely cut ties with those same friends.

Amidst all this, I discovered a source of happiness in my life - Star Wars. Spending time on the internet, I found solace in a galaxy far, far away. Collecting single issue editions of the Darth Vader comic books became my passion, and I would travel for hours to add them to my collection. This quest kept my mind focused, and it felt like I was on a mission to find my own treasure. I also immersed myself in reading the old novels and watching the movies. Although I was on a leave of absence from my Walmart job, I had Personal Time Off to fall back on, so my finances were not a worry for a while.

However, despite all this, I still felt an emptiness inside me. It was as if I was disconnected from reality and from God. No matter what I did, I felt unwanted and excluded by people around me.

The thought of ending my own life kept recurring in my mind. When you feel utterly alone and defeated, suicide can seem like the only escape. When you believe that the weight of the world is on your shoulders and everything is crumbling down, it can crush even the happiest of people. I realized that I don't fear death, but rather the thought of being alone.

Despite these dark thoughts, I refused to give in. I knew I had to fight and not let myself slip away. However, I couldn't always keep it together and eventually, I succumbed to my struggles.

It's important to note that thinking that suicide is the only solution is a harmful and incorrect way of thinking. If you find yourself in this situation, it's essential to seek help. Mental health services are now more accessible than ever before. In 2023, you can even receive assistance from mental health apps like BetterHelp if you're struggling. You must not let your emotions take control of your life. Your life is worth more than anything, and it's crucial to realize that. Looking back, I wish I had known this, but at the same time, I was strong-willed enough to keep pushing forward.

The Dark Descent:

My Journey Through Anger and Violence

During this period, as I mentioned earlier, I was taking Xanax. As time passed, I started to develop a liking for the drug. Feeling sad? Take a pill. Feeling angry? Take a pill. Feeling lonely? Take two more pills. At one point, I was so short on money that I was willing to sell my belongings, not to buy more pills, but because my funds for school were almost depleted, and I was on medical leave from work. So, I resorted to pawning off some of my most prized possessions.

There were several days when I was heavily relying on Xanax, and during one of those days, I went to a pawn shop with my long-time friend and her brother to sell my Peavey Jf-1 guitar. We had already been to two other pawn shops, and I was feeling frustrated after unsuccessfully trying to sell my AR-15. As we waited in line, my anger was building up, and by the time we got to the counter, I was on the verge of exploding. When the pawnshop offered me a measly $42 for my guitar, which they would resell for $580, I lost control and slammed everything on the counter to the ground. Even though the deal was not favorable, my behavior was unacceptable. The pawnshop threatened to call the police, and I stormed out of the store while cursing out the workers. Looking back, I regret my actions, as I not only put my friends in a difficult situation but also caused unnecessary chaos for the pawnshop employees who did not deserve it.

I am sad to say that this kind of explosive anger, which originated from that time, still plagues me to some extent. It's not as severe as it used to be, but it's still a problem that I'm working on. I've come to realize that taking Xanax as a way to deal with my emotions was not a healthy solution, and it only served to exacerbate my anger and violent tendencies.

Through therapy and counseling, I've learned to manage my emotions in healthier ways, such as through meditation and mindfulness practices. It's a slow and ongoing process, but I am hopeful that with time and dedication, I can overcome this negative aspect of myself and become a better person for it.

My behavior was not only affecting my relationships with my family but also with my friends. I would snap at them for small things and push them away when they tried to help me. I became isolated and felt like nobody understood me or what I was going through. The more I pushed people away, the more alone and angry I felt. It was a vicious cycle, and I couldn't seem to break free from it. It took me a long time to realize that the only person responsible for my behavior was me, and I needed to take control of it. It's still a struggle, but I'm working hard to become a better person and learn healthier ways to deal with my emotions.

But this was only half of my rage. When I was alone, it was much worse. I would get enraged by the littlest stuff and hurt myself. I remember one night when I slammed my face into the wall repeatedly because I was angry at a video game. And then there was the time when I punched myself in the face until my nose bled profusely when I got mad at my car. Honestly, I cannot tell you why I had gotten so self-destructive. It would end up making me even madder because I would hurt myself, fueling my rage. I began to hate myself and God, thinking he was enjoying my suffering. I saw this unknown benevolent figure as just watching a sick ant twitch around on the ground, like a child who just hurt it. Looking back, I can laugh, but I was serious. I began to use pain as punishment on myself. If I felt I did something wrong, I'd end up hurting myself. My mental health was deteriorating fast. Reality to me was nothing but a concept that I could not understand. Why were all these bad things happening to me? What could I have done to deserve what was being dealt with me? One night I was driving home, and I thought a car was following me, so I began to drive a little dangerously, swerving quickly into turns, car tires squalling. Each time a new car would appear, I would think it was the same people. So I ended up pulling over and getting out and just standing there, probably confusing the driver, but they drove past, and in my mind, I was in the clear. I was never rational in these situations; I just knew I was mad and paranoid. I would never hurt anyone, though. When I was in this frame of mind, I believed I was superior to that.

I realize now that my actions were not healthy, nor were they healthy ways to cope. Taking Xanax to numb my emotions and self-harming when I felt angry or frustrated was only hurting myself even more. In the moment, it felt like a release, but the temporary relief was followed by more pain and anger. It's not okay to hurt myself or others when I am feeling overwhelmed or upset. I know now that there are healthier ways to cope, such as talking to a therapist, journaling, or doing activities that bring me joy and relaxation. It's important for me to recognize when I am feeling overwhelmed and to take a step back to find healthy ways to deal with my emotions instead of lashing out.

Eventually, I realized that relying on Xanax was not a healthy coping mechanism for my anger and depression. While I can't place full blame on the medication, as I still experienced uncontrollable outbursts even after stopping it, I knew that continuing to rely on it wasn't a sustainable solution. However, getting off the medication was difficult because my anxiety returned, and I struggled with insomnia. I had become so accustomed to the way Xanax made me feel that it was hard to let go. One night, something triggered me, and I completely denounced my faith in God. It was a way to hurt him if he was there and punish him for what I perceived as him punishing me. As the weeks went by, I went back to the specialist and met with a new doctor. They did the same breathing exercises to see if they had improved, but they hadn't. I felt enraged and began to hate everyone and everything, including myself and God. It wasn't a healthy way to cope, and I knew that I needed to find better ways to manage my anger and depression.

I was angry with the Dr S's office in particular. I tried to rationalize and make sense of their behavior. Maybe they were just trying to make more money off of me. They would give my parents dirty

looks and were consistently rude to us. It felt like the doctor was trying to belittle us. This continued for about a month until it was January and I was called back into the office. The doctor said, "Well, we still do not understand why this is happening, but your most recent x-ray and CT scan show that the fluid is returning."
I could feel the heat rising in my face.
I asked him, "How?"

"That's what we plan to find out," he replied. "We'll put in a chest tube and set a small camera inside it to look around the outside of the lung. This will help us make sure there are no tumors or tears on the lung. The surgery is simple and shouldn't take more than an hour or two."

A thoracoscopy, also known as video-assisted thoracoscopic surgery (VATS), is a minimally invasive surgical procedure used to diagnose and treat problems in the chest, particularly in the lungs and the lining of the chest wall.

During a thoracoscopy, a surgeon makes a small incision in the chest and inserts a tiny camera called a thoracoscope, along with surgical instruments, through the incision. The camera allows the surgeon to see the inside of the chest on a video monitor, which helps guide the surgery. The surgeon can then perform various procedures, such as taking a biopsy, removing fluid or tissue, or repairing damaged tissue.

VATS is considered less invasive than traditional open surgery, which requires a larger incision and can cause more pain and a longer recovery time. Because VATS involves smaller incisions, it may result in less pain, less scarring, and a shorter recovery time.

"Okay," I responded, feeling drained from the whole ordeal.

"I want to see you again in two weeks," the doctor stated.

"Got it," I replied, relieved to have a set timeframe.

Leaving the doctor's office that day, I couldn't help but feel a glimmer of hope. With two weeks until my surgery, I decided to use that time to focus on spending quality time with my family.

During the two weeks leading up to my surgery, instead of spending time with my family, I found myself withdrawing into my room. I would listen to the same record player I had received for Christmas two years prior and feel an overwhelming sense of loneliness. Despite my parents and brother inviting me to do things with them and his girlfriend, I refused to join them. I didn't want to be the third wheel and felt more isolated than ever. Thoughts of suicide became a constant obsession for me, and death seemed like the only way out. I considered ending my life while my parents were in the living room, completely unaware, or waiting until they returned home from somewhere to discover my lifeless body. I even imagined leaving a note behind, apologizing for the pain I caused and explaining that death was the only way out for me. Looking back now, I see how sick and twisted my thoughts were. It was like I had two separate faces - the happy-go-lucky kid I showed to the world, and the sad, hateful, and self-destructive person I kept hidden inside. I started feeling empty, and as time went on, that emptiness turned into numbness. I stopped caring about anything and everything, and even though I slept all the time, it wasn't because I was tired. I was just lonely.

As a 24-year-old man reflecting back on my 19-year-old self, I can see how sad and lonely I truly was. Reading my own words now, it's heartbreaking to think of the pain I was going through. But I want this account to serve as a reminder that things do get better. Even though it may feel like the weight of the world is on your shoulders, there is always hope for a brighter tomorrow.

If this book can change even one person's life, then I will have accomplished what I set out to do. I've written other books since this one, but none of them hold the same impact for me. This book is different because it's personal, it's raw, and it speaks to the struggles that so many of us face at one point or another.

If you're going through a tough time, my advice to you is this: don't give up. It may sound cliché, but it's true. Life is a journey, and sometimes the road is bumpy. But you are strong enough to face whatever comes your way. Don't be afraid to reach out for help, whether it's from a friend, a family member, or a professional. Remember, you are not alone. There is hope, and there is a light at the end of the tunnel. Keep pushing forward, and you will come out on top.

Into Thin Air:
My Journey through a Thoracoscopy

After wasting weeks wallowing in self-pity and hopelessness, the day of my surgery had finally arrived. The night before, I was instructed not to eat or drink anything after eleven o'clock at night to avoid any complications during the anesthesia or surgery. I certainly didn't want to risk waking up in the middle of the operation or a misdiagnosis. The next morning, I took a shower and packed my bags, knowing that this would be my first time staying in a hospital. I made sure to bring a few books to keep myself entertained during recovery, including two Star Wars novels: "Into the Void: Star Wars Legends" and "Star Wars: The Old Republic - Revan".

As my parents and I arrived at Fort Hamilton Hospital in Hamilton, Ohio, I noticed the massive Christmas tree still standing outside the building, singing its cheerful tunes. Although I couldn't help but appreciate the beauty of the tree, part of me couldn't help but think of the Grinch's evil antics in the classic movie "How the Grinch Stole Christmas." I chuckled at the thought and walked inside with my parents. As we approached the sign-in area, I couldn't help but feel a wave of nervousness wash over me.

We settled into the waiting area until the nurse returned and directed us to a familiar small room. As I sat down on the bed, I felt a sense of resignation to the process. The nurse instructed me to remove my earrings, even the newly pierced one on my upper ear lobe, which annoyed me. I reluctantly took them out and changed into the blue gown they provided. Lying down under the covers, my parents joined me in the room and we chatted nervously, trying to ease the tension. Suddenly, there was a knock on the wall outside and I invited the doctor in.

The doctor approached me just before the procedure was set to begin. Unlike the previous doctor, he was kind and reassuring. "Kyle, there's no need to be nervous. The procedure is quite simple. We'll be inserting a tube into your chest on the left side to drain any remaining fluid, and we'll be able to examine the area with a small camera," he explained. Trying to sound confident, I replied, "Alright, I'm ready." But inside, my legs felt like jelly and my stomach was in knots. Thankfully, the nurse returned and hooked up a saline bag to my bed, which helped alleviate my hunger pains. After saying goodbye to my parents, she wheeled me towards the large doors.

As she scanned her badge, the doors opened with a loud click. A blast of icy air hit my face as we turned left and stopped in front of a door that read "Operating Room" in bold red letters. The nurse pushed the doors open, and the cold air rushed in again, making my lungs ache. I was then lifted onto the operating table, and the bright fluorescent lights blinded me once more. It was like something out of an alien abduction movie, with masked nurses looming over me. It was eerie, and in hindsight, a bit unsettling. The anesthesiologist I had met earlier walked in and asked for my information again before we began. They hooked me up to an IV and the anesthesia immediately took over my body.

As the anesthesia kicked in, I started rambling about anything and everything that popped into my head. I fixated on the clock across from me, daydreaming about traveling to the future. My speech became slurred as the medication took hold, until eventually, I couldn't speak anymore. The lights were still on, but it felt like nobody was home. Finally, they placed a mask over my face and everything went black.

Upon regaining consciousness, I found myself in a new room, surrounded by curtains and in excruciating pain. My entire body was itchy for some reason, and I found myself reciting Edgar Allan Poe's "The Raven." With my eyes still closed, I was unaware of anyone else in the room with me until a woman's voice spoke up beside me.

"Are you reciting poetry?" she asked.

I responded groggily, "Yeah," and continued reciting. "Come here and listen to this."

She chuckled and spoke to someone else, but I was too disoriented to make out what they were saying.

Fentanyl is a powerful synthetic opioid pain medication that is commonly used to treat severe pain, particularly in cancer patients or for post-surgical pain management. It works by binding to opioid receptors in the brain and spinal cord, which reduces the sensation of pain. However, one of the side effects of fentanyl is itchiness or skin irritation, which can be a result of histamine release in the body. This is known as opioid-induced pruritus and can be a common side effect of fentanyl use.

I remained with my eyes closed, feeling the persistent itching sensation all over my body, trying to make sense of my surroundings. Soon after, I dozed off again. When I opened my eyes, I was still groggy and disoriented. Suddenly, a nurse walked in. She had dark hair, different from the nurse I had heard earlier. She approached me and said,

"Oh, you're awake! Can I get you anything?"

I inquired, "Why am I feeling so itchy right now?"

The nurse replied, "It's a common side effect of anesthesia. I'll get you some Benadryl."

After she left, she returned shortly with a cup of ice chips and two small pills of Benadryl. I took them and drifted back to sleep. The next time I woke up, I was more alert and aware of the pain in my chest. I groaned in discomfort and one of the nurses called out to me.

"I got your pain medicine," she said, handing me a small cup with some pills and water. "Take these and try to relax. The pain should subside soon."
I nodded and swallowed the pills, feeling a wave of relief wash over me. My dad held my hand as I leaned back against the pillows, staring at the ceiling.
"You did great, bugs," he said, his voice filled with pride.
I managed a weak smile and closed my eyes, feeling exhausted and drained. The nurse checked on me periodically, adjusting the IV and

checking the tube in my side. The pain gradually subsided and I drifted in and out of sleep, feeling groggy and disoriented.

"I'll get you some pain medicine," the nurse said. As she left, the curtain was pulled back and my dad walked in. "Looking good, bugs," he said with a smile. Bugs was the nickname my family called me. I smiled back and sat up a little.

"Be careful, you have a big tube sticking out your side," he warned me, noticing the giant straw-like tube protruding from my side. Liquid was flowing out of it with every breath. I was taken aback by its size. The nurse returned with a cup of pills and a small cup of water with ice chips.

"What kind of pain killer is this?" I asked before taking them.

"Percocet," she replied.

The mention of the drug made me hesitant, as it was the pill I had become addicted to after my hernia surgery a year before. But the pain was too intense, and I had to take them. My dad pulled up a chair and sat down.

"Where's mom?" I asked.

"She ran home to get a few things," he replied. The Percocet began to take effect, and my body became numb. The pain dissipated, and I let the medication take over.

As I drifted in and out of consciousness, I heard another nurse say, "The patient who just got the chest tube has been ordered for immediate transport to Kettering Hospital. We have to get an ambulance later. Let me call over to Kettering to see if they have any available rooms."

After hearing about the sudden transportation plan, my stomach sank. The original plan was for me to stay at Fort Hamilton hospital for a

day or two after my surgery. I glanced over at my dad, hoping for some answers. Just then, the nurse walked back in. I couldn't contain my curiosity and asked, "Why am I being transported?"
She replied, "I'm not entirely sure." "Don't worry, Kyle. You're fine. He's just a worry-wart," said my dad.
Despite my dad's attempt to ease my worry, I couldn't shake the feeling that something was off. However, the effects of the Percocet had kicked in, and I was too numb to care. Suddenly, I felt a tingling sensation in my abdomen - I needed to pee.
"I have to go to the bathroom," I told the nurse.
She handed me a urinal, but I asked if I could walk to the bathroom instead. However, she reminded me that I was connected to several machines and couldn't get up. My dad stepped out, and the nurse helped me stand up. As she handed me the urinal, I mustered up the courage to ask, "Could you maybe step out? I'm a little gun shy." But even with privacy, I still couldn't pee.

After ten minutes, I finally urinated and laid back down. When the nurse returned, she inquired, "So what exactly happened? You had pneumonia? And then what?"
"Well, I guess I had fluid around my lung and they had to check for anything on the outside of my lung. I had a bronchoscopy that showed I was clear of anything on the inside," I explained.
"That's strange. This is the procedure older people undergo, not a 19-year-old kid. Did you smoke?" she asked.
"Yeah, but I quit two or three months ago," I replied.
"Good," she nodded before leaving me to rest. My mom arrived and we chatted for a while. Just then, the nurse got a phone call and walked back into my hospital room.

At around eight o'clock at night, the nurse informed us that a spot had opened up at Kettering Hospital and that we would have to wait for the ambulance to arrive for transportation. When the ambulance finally showed up, I was disconnected from all my wiring and my bed was pushed up to the stretcher with my chest tube and its fluid box. Strapped down like a crazy person in a straitjacket, I was pushed by the medical staff, with my parents beside me.
"We'll meet you at the other hospital. I love you," my mom said.
"Love you, bugs. You're gonna be all right," my dad said.

"Love you too," I replied.

As we made our way down the corridor towards the ambulance waiting outside, the bitter cold air made it difficult to breathe, and my chest continued to burn. I remember the snow falling gently outside. As they opened the doors and wheeled me in, the journey to Kettering became a blur. All I could do was hope that we wouldn't skid off the icy road. I don't recall arriving at the hospital, only waking up in a hospital room sometime later. The next morning, the nurse woke me up and brought me water and Percocet, which I had apparently requested. My mother had spent the night sleeping in a chair next to my bed. The nurse returned a little later and informed me, "Dr. S says you need to have your chest tube removed, so we'll do that and then he'll come to speak with you."

The nurse arrived with a few supplies - rags, scissors, and bandages. Instructing me to lie on my right side away from the chest tube, she said, "Let's do a practice run before we remove it. Hold your breath and grunt as hard as you can." After practicing, she prepared the area with paper towels and started removing the staples, causing a pinching sensation. Then she asked, "Ready?" and pulled out the tube. The scraping of the tube against my rib made me feel like my stomach was being squeezed, and I felt a burning sensation at the site. I moaned in pain, feeling sick and my eyes swimming. The nurse put the bloody end of the tube in a biohazard bag and bandaged me up. When she finished, I turned back over onto my back, shaking profusely. My mom tried to cheer me up by saying, "See, that was fast."

I glared at my mom, my frustration with her still lingering from our earlier conversation. The pain that had just shot through my body was so intense and sudden that it felt like it was burning itself into my mind. I had experienced stomach aches before, but this was something entirely different. My chest felt like it was on fire, throbbing with each heartbeat.

As I tried to catch my breath and calm my racing heart, there was a knock on the door. I managed to say, "Come in," and a new doctor stepped into the room. He introduced himself, I don't remember his name so ill refer to him as Dr. Blank and explained that Dr. S had sent me to him because of a troubling discovery during my last surgery.

Dr. Blank shuffled through some papers before revealing the source of the trouble: a large mass connecting my lung to my chest wall. The sight of the mass made my stomach churn. It was bloody, with black spots dotting its surface.

My heart racing again, I asked the question that had been on my mind since seeing the mass, "Is it a tumor?" I handed the paper over to my mom, hoping she would understand my fear.

Dr. Blank shook his head, "As of right now, we're not sure. It might be an empyema, which is where a collection of pus pushes out of the lung." My mind raced with the possibilities of what this could mean for my health and my future.

He continued to explain, "But judging by what we've talked to your doctors about, we aren't exactly sure what to classify your case as yet. It's not anything bacterial or viral, judging by your blood-work and Pleurisy tests."

I frowned in confusion and frustration, "That makes little sense."

"Exactly. So what we will do is what we call a thoracotomy. That's where we make a small cut under your shoulder blade to get to your lung and the mass. We're going to get that mass out of there because it is causing your lung to tear and bleed. Hence, bloody pleurisy. The procedure of cutting the mass out is what we call a decortication. It's an invasive surgery and will take a few hours."

My mind was racing with all the new information. This was a lot to process all at once. I had come to the hospital expecting to recover from my previous surgery, not to hear about another one. And this would be my fourth surgery in just two months. It was overwhelming.

I looked over at my mom and saw the shock and concern in her eyes, mirroring my own.

"I have a procedure I have to do in thirty minutes. If I get finished a little early, I'd like to start immediately," the doctor said.

"So I will get back ahold of you comes up." With that, he finished and walked out. I sat there in silence, feeling a mix of pain and disappointment. The thought of yet another surgery made my heart ache and tears started to stream down my face. Could my body handle the pain that was about to come? I wasn't so sure.

My mom tried to comfort me, saying, "You'll be okay, whatever will be, will be. God will help you."

I couldn't help but scoff at her words. "Yeah, right," I thought bitterly. "Do you really think I'm just going to sit here and beg for mercy? Pray and hope for the best? Not a chance."

I had so much hatred towards God now. The idea of just 'praying' and waiting for something to happen without taking any action seemed like wishful thinking to me. It was something people did to make themselves feel better. And whether something good or bad happened, they would simply attribute it to God's reasoning. But I had a problem, and I was determined to face it with or without any divine intervention. After a few hours had passed, it was finally nighttime, and I went to bed. The next morning, a nurse came in and said, "Your procedure is scheduled for twelve o'clock. Normally we hand out menus, but seeing how you have surgery in two hours, that's not such a good idea." I nodded, and she gave me my medicine. It was just my mom and me again. "I'm nervous," I said, glancing over at her. "Why, bugs?" she asked.

"Because all this stuff is happening to me, and I don't know why. They're telling me they don't know what's wrong with me, and it's driving me insane. I feel like I have no control over this situation, and it will only get worse."

"We all go through things sometimes, but it's up to us to let it affect us or not," she replied. "So don't worry about it, just watch some TV or get some sleep. Your Uncle Rob is coming here soon to see you."

I drifted off to sleep, exhaustion taking over my body. When I awoke, my Uncle was sitting beside me, a smile spreading across his face. We talked for a while, catching up on old times, but time seemed to slip away from us.

Suddenly, it was time for my fourth surgery. I knew this was it - my awakening. The anticipation built up inside me as I was wheeled into the operating room.

Despite the many questions unanswered and my hopes being continually thwarted, I remembered my mother's words. It was up to me to let this experience either bother me or take control of my life. I decided to let go of everything and not let this situation overpower me.

It wasn't easy. The pain and misery I endured were overwhelming at times, and I questioned why this was happening to me. But now, looking back, I am grateful for this experience. Sometimes, we have to go through hell to get to heaven.

Split Open:
My Journey through a Life-Saving Thoracotomy

A sharp knock echoed through the room, and my heart raced in anticipation. Two nurses entered, their voices echoing with a professional but reassuring tone.

"Okay, Mr. Combs, we'll take you down now. Dr. (Blank) is ready to see you," they said, glancing over at me with practiced smiles.

Turning to my mom and uncle, I forced a brave face. "I'll see you guys later," I said, my voice quivering slightly. My mother's eyes held a glint of worry, but she tried to hide it with a confident smile. My uncle's expression was more stoic, but his words were just as reassuring. "You'll be okay," he said.

But deep down, I was lying to myself. Fear coiled inside me, tightening with each passing moment. As they wheeled me down the corridor, the world seemed to blur around me, and I struggled to maintain my composure.

At the end of the hall was an elevator, unlike any I had seen before. Its grandeur was reminiscent of something out of Charlie and the Chocolate Factory, with its size and intricate details. We descended down, and as we approached our destination, the air grew colder and colder.

As they pushed me into the room, I noticed the curtains lining the walls. Each one seemed to hold a patient within, all hidden away from prying eyes. They wheeled me into an empty space, and I felt a shiver run down my spine as they locked the bed down and began to walk away.

My heart was racing as I took in my surroundings, struggling to contain my anxiety. The room was sterile and cold, filled with the smell of disinfectant and the hum of medical equipment. I glanced up at the nurses with a mix of fear and disbelief.

"Surely they aren't doing the surgery here!" I blurted out.

The nurses chuckled softly, their eyes kind but knowing. "No, no," one of them said, "this is just the prep area. We have to go get the anesthesiologist."

My heart sank as I realized what was to come. Moments later, a bearded man entered the room, pushing a cart filled with medical supplies. He approached me with a gentle smile, but his words were anything but comforting.

"What's up, man," he said. "I'm gonna suggest you do this before the procedure because a thoracotomy is one of the most painful things to go through."

My mind reeled as he spoke, the reality of the situation sinking in. He continued, his tone matter-of-fact as he outlined the procedure.

"So I'm going to highly recommend you do an epidural. Is that all right with you? All we have to do is numb the area and stick a needle in between an area in your spine. This may cause back pain and terrible headaches but that's unlikely."

I felt a lump form in my throat as I nodded, the fear almost too much to bear. But I knew what had to be done, no matter how painful the road ahead.

"I'll do anything to prevent further pain," I declared firmly. With that, the anesthesiologist went ahead and numbed the area. My hands were placed across a table as they had been for the thoracentesis, and I braced myself as the needle was inserted. The nurse held my arms steady in case of any sudden movements. When it was all over, they unlocked the wheels, and we made our way towards two large doors that read "Operation Room" in bold letters.

As we entered, the stark contrast from the Fort Hamilton room was immediately apparent. The room was pristine, every surface a blinding white, illuminated by harsh fluorescent lighting. The doctors and nurses were dressed in white, their mint green masks covering their faces. The machines surrounding me looked like they were straight out of a science fiction movie, beeping and booping with an otherworldly rhythm. For a fleeting moment, I entertained a bizarre thought - what if this wasn't an operation, but some kind of secret government experiment?

Shaking off the wild idea, I was lifted onto the operation table, a flimsy gown draped over me. Suddenly, I realized that I was completely exposed, and with a blush rising to my cheeks, I quickly crossed my legs.

As I crossed my legs, a nurse yanked them apart, scolding me, "You can't cross your legs." I couldn't help but make a joke, trying to ease my nerves. "Well, I just didn't want you to see my junk, but I'm sure you see them every day. And I'm sure some of them are a lot better looking than mine." The room burst into laughter, and for a moment, I forgot where I was. The surgeon strolled in and everyone in the room seemed to be buzzing with excitement, cheering him on and cracking jokes. Meanwhile, I was lying there, exposed and vulnerable. He approached me and tried to reassure me, "All right, today's the day you have nothing to be worried about-" But before he could finish, the anesthetics in my IV line started to take effect. Suddenly, the room seemed more lively, and I felt more sociable. As he placed the mask over my nose and mouth, he added, "Just think, when you wake up, you're gonna be all better." I couldn't resist one last quip, "So you're not gonna ship me off as the other one did?" The room erupted into laughter once more, and then everything went dark.

As I slowly came to, the searing pain in my chest was unbearable. Every breath felt like fire and I couldn't help but moan in agony. My lips were stuck together in a grimace, giving me an eerie Joker-like smile. I felt like I was on the verge of passing out from the intensity of the pain. In my delirium, I even begged for death to end my suffering. I sensed something spraying into my nose and realized it was a hose from an oxygen tank. My breaths were shallow, and every exhale turned into a whistling wheeze.

Suddenly, I felt a strange sensation, like I was urinating. I fumbled my hands down to investigate, and to my horror, I felt a cord sticking out. My mind raced with wild thoughts. Was I some kind of experiment gone wrong? Had I been turned into a monster and stashed away in some secret facility?

But as I opened my eyes, I saw that I was in a small, dimly lit room. There were wires and machines everywhere, beeping and whirring in a chaotic symphony. I realized I was in the ICU, hooked up to more machines than I could count.

Just then, an elderly nurse entered the room. I tried to speak, but my voice was barely a whisper.

I croaked out, "Water...Please. My mouth is so... dry." The nurse smiled and said, "Right away hun."

Moments later, she returned with the water. As I took a sip, I couldn't help but think about the value we put on things. Diamonds are expensive, but water is essential for life and yet we waste it without a second thought. I savored each drop of the cool liquid, grateful for its refreshing taste.

Just then, my mom and uncle walked into the room. "Hey, bugs. How are you feeling?" my mom asked with concern etched on her face.

I struggled to speak, "Look at me." She chuckled and said, "I'm gonna head home. I can stay if you want me to."

"No. I'll be fine... I'm just going to sleep," I whispered, feeling exhausted from the pain and medication.

"Okay, well, I'll come back tomorrow. Call me if you need anything," she said, giving me a kiss on the forehead before leaving.

As I slowly regained consciousness, I became aware of a strange feeling of disorientation. My mind was still foggy and my body felt heavy. Then, as I looked around the room, I realized that something was missing - my phone. I beckoned the nurse over and asked her to retrieve it from the far end of the room. Once she had handed it to me, I placed it within reach and felt a small sense of relief wash over me.

My mother and uncle had visited earlier, and I remembered their voices as they said their goodbyes. As I lay there, I felt my eyelids grow heavy once more and drifted back to sleep. However, my slumber was short-lived as I was abruptly awakened again, this time by a group of nurses who were moving me.

As I was being wheeled through the hospital corridors, I heard a cacophony of screams and laughter echoing off the walls. The sound grew louder as we got closer to our destination, and I could tell that it was coming from the psych-ward on the same floor. I couldn't help but wonder, "Where am I?" as we passed through the unfamiliar hallways.

As I opened my eyes, I heard a man's piercing screams that sounded like they were straight out of a horror movie. But as we moved further away, the noise faded into the background. It was the same sterile hospital room I had been in before, only this time with a different nurse attending to me. I reached for my phone to check the time and saw that it was already eight in the morning. When I looked at the window, I saw the faint light of daybreak filtering through the curtains. I realized that I hadn't seen the outside world in two days, and my sense of time was completely off.

Suddenly, a sharp pain in my chest jolted me to full consciousness. I looked down and saw two hoses sticking out of my side, draining a red fluid into a box labeled "biohazard." The hospital staff had hooked it up to a dolly and placed my catheter bag, which had been inserted through my groin, on the same cart. I tried to sit up using the controls on the bed and felt a series of grooves along my back, which were from the incision they made during my surgery.

As I looked around for something to ease the pain, I noticed a remote control on the bedside table that I hadn't seen before. I reached for it, hoping it was a call button for the nurses, and pressed it. Suddenly, a deafening beep followed by an unfamiliar sound echoed from a machine above me. To my surprise, the cooling sensation in my chest felt like water dousing a fire, thanks to the epidural they had administered. However, I also felt a wet spot forming on my shoulder, and I realized that the machine had caused me to sweat.

Desperately needing some relief, I searched for the real button to call the nurse and finally found it on the remote. When the nurse answered, I whispered, "Is it medicine time?" while holding the remote close to my face.

"Yes, I was actually just about to head down there," she replied.

As the nurse arrived with my medication, I eagerly awaited the relief that it would bring. She handed me a small plastic cup containing pills and a diet Pepsi. I swallowed the pills, hoping they would dull the pain that radiated throughout my body. It wasn't long before the medication took effect and I drifted off into a peaceful sleep.

When I woke up, my parents and uncle were by my side. Despite the medication, I still felt sore and tears streamed down my face. My dad asked me how I was feeling and I couldn't help but let out a sob. The Percocet made it difficult to control my emotions and the tears only added to my discomfort.

As my mom tried to console me, I cried out in frustration. "This is no way to live," I lamented. But every time I cried, it felt like daggers piercing through my chest, intensifying the pain I was feeling.

My mom tried to offer words of encouragement, saying that the pain was only temporary and that I would feel much better once I was out of the hospital. But at that moment, all I could focus on was the agony that consumed me, making it hard to see any light at the end of the tunnel.

As I lay in my hospital bed, I couldn't believe the excruciating pain that consumed my chest with every breath I took. It was a new level of agony that I had never experienced before. Even the simplest tasks, like talking or moving, felt like a Herculean feat. I tossed and turned, trying to get comfortable, but sleep eluded me. My heart rate began to rise, and before I knew it, I was in the middle of a full-blown panic attack. I knew I needed something to calm me down, so I asked for Xanax. The familiar relief it provided was more soothing than any form of affection I had ever known.

My mother stayed by my side, dozing off occasionally. But for me, sleep was impossible. Thoughts and worries raced through my mind, and the surgeon's lack of communication only fueled my anxiety. I couldn't help but conjure up worst-case scenarios, which only made things worse. And so, I continued to ask for more Xanax to help me cope.

As the hours ticked by, I found myself lost in an Al Pacino movie marathon. But as I watched Carlito's Way, a scene where Al's character has his lawyer shot in the chest hit me hard. It was as if I could feel the pain shooting through my own chest, and my mind began to play tricks on me. I couldn't help but wonder, "Is this what it feels like to get shot in the chest?"

The morning came, and I was still wide awake when the third shift nurses left and the first shift arrived. My mom woke up and got me some breakfast, but I could barely eat. My body was wasting away; I had lost so much weight that my face had sunken in, and my cheeks were hollow. The nurse came in and gave me a shot in the stomach to prevent blood clots, and that was when I met one of the male nurses, an African American man who was always kind to me and made me laugh, even when it hurt too much to do so.

But it wasn't just the physical pain that was difficult to endure; it was the emotional pain of not being able to laugh or enjoy anything anymore. The pain was so intense that I would end up crying, which only made things worse. Eventually, though, I learned how to clear my mind and find some peace.

That night, my dad came to visit, but he ended up sleeping in the car because the pain was too much for him to bear. I lay there, once again wide awake and in agony, pushing the epidural button for relief. Eventually, I drifted off to sleep, only to be woken up by an old man named Harold, who had come to pray with me as part of the hospital's religious group.

Looking back on those difficult days, I realize how much I owe to the kindness of the people who crossed my path. One of them was Harold, an old man who came to my hospital room to pray with me. At the time, I didn't fully appreciate the gesture, but now I see how much comfort and hope it brought me.

As I reflect on that time, a Bible verse comes to mind: "And we know that in all things God works for the good of those who love him, who have been called according to his purpose." (Romans 8:28)

This verse speaks to the idea that even in the midst of pain and suffering, there is a higher purpose at work. It reminds us that God is always with us and that he can bring good out of any situation.

In my case, I can see how this verse played out in my life. Despite the pain and uncertainty, I received care and compassion from the medical staff, my family, and even strangers like Harold. Through it all, I learned to appreciate the little moments of kindness and connection that made a big difference in my journey towards healing.

As I listened to the man's words, I felt a twinge of curiosity in my chest. I nodded in agreement as he spoke, wondering to myself, "What have I got to lose?" Suddenly, he reached out and took my hands in his, and I closed my eyes as he began to pray. I felt a strange sensation wash over me, a feeling of pure bliss and ecstasy that I hadn't experienced in years. And then, out of nowhere, a thought invaded my mind: "He's still here."

I knew exactly what that thought meant. It meant that the God I had once hated and denounced was still listening, still present in my life. When the man finished praying, I thanked him and he left, but I couldn't stop thinking about the experience. Throughout my entire life, I had faced countless hardships, but I had never felt truly alone. I had always had someone to confide in, whether it was a friend, a family member, or now, God.

I had heard people say that we're supposed to have a relationship with God like we have with our friends, but I had never truly understood what that meant until now. In that moment, my life changed forever. I felt a sense of purpose and direction that I had never felt before, and I knew that I had to follow it.

But at the same time, I also realized something else. Before I could truly love someone else, I had to learn to love myself. And that was the one thing I still struggled with - hating myself. But with God's help, I knew that I could overcome that, too. In just that instant, my life had flipped upside down, but I had a newfound light paving my way forward.

During my stay at Kettering Hospital, I endured a grueling experience that took a toll on both my mind and body. My muscles ached and I was consumed with a sense of bitterness. However, there was one male nurse who I found myself connecting with. He shared with me the devastating news that his wife had recently passed away, and my heart went out to him.

As I listened to his story, I realized something that had never occurred to me before. I had always been aware that there were other people around me, but I had never truly seen them as individuals with their own unique lives and experiences. It was almost as if I viewed people as a collective entity rather than as individuals with their own stories to tell.

But as I spoke with this nurse, I began to comprehend just how complex and diverse every person's life truly is. It was a revelation that left me feeling somewhat stunned. So many people, so many lives, each with their own joys and sorrows. It was a humbling realization that helped me to see people in a new light - as individuals with their own hopes, dreams, and struggles.

I'm not a psychologist, but I can try to explain the psychology behind my experiences. Throughout school, I felt isolated and disconnected from others. Although I had friends, I didn't feel as though I truly belonged in any particular group. This left me with low self-esteem and a fear of rejection.

I think my fear of rejection stemmed from my negative self-image. I didn't view myself as equal to my friends, and I believed that others wouldn't view me in a positive light either. This negative self-talk became a vicious cycle that reinforced my negative beliefs about myself and led to further isolation.

I also had a belief that everything was fake and that people weren't truly my friends. I think this was a defense mechanism to protect myself from potential rejection or disappointment. However, it prevented me from forming deeper connections with others and experiencing the benefits of meaningful relationships.

Overall, my experiences in school had a significant impact on my self-esteem and sense of belonging. I think it would be helpful to explore these experiences further with a mental health professional to better understand how they have influenced my life and relationships.

To be honest, I would be lying if I said that I have completely grown out of my negative tendencies. I have hurt many people in my life, including friends, family, and even strangers. For a long time, I only attracted negative people into my life because, as they say, "negatives attract negatives."

One of the best friends I ever had was someone I hurt deeply. I lied to her and hurt her in many ways, and I regret it all now that I have cleared my mind, detoxed, and found God. But in many ways, she did the same to me. I didn't truly know her, and she lied, hurt, and shamed me for years before I had enough. However, the way I handled it was completely wrong. Instead of showing mutual respect and just cutting ties in the right way, I insulted her, judged her life choices, and hurt and ridiculed her.

Now I realize how hurt and broken she was even before I came into her life. I don't want anything bad to happen to her, but I can't be around her because of her negative energy. The reason I mention this is that you would think that when I originally wrote this book, I would have learned my lesson about forgiveness. But sometimes, God sends us messages multiple times before we can truly understand.

In Matthew 6:14-15, it says, "For if you forgive other people when they sin against you, your heavenly Father will also forgive you. But if you do not forgive others their sins, your Father will not forgive your sins." This verse teaches us the importance of forgiving those who have hurt us, even if they don't deserve it. It's not always easy, but it's necessary for our own emotional and spiritual well-being.

In this situation, I realize that my friend was hurting and broken, just like me. Instead of judging her and hurting her more, I should have shown her kindness, love, and forgiveness. I hope that someday we can both find healing and forgiveness, even if we can't be in each other's lives.

From Scarred to Strong: My Journey Home after Thoracotomy

After four days in the hospital, my parents filled me in on what the outside world looked like. I had undergone a thoracotomy and needed respiration therapy because there was a hole in my lung. Breathing caused bubbling sensations in my chest due to the mass that was removed cutting into my lung. Though weak, I managed to lift myself out of bed with some effort. The surgeon arrived that afternoon with the results; it was negative, which brought a wave of relief, but they still didn't know the root cause. Later that evening, I met with the respiration therapist and began a breathing exercise routine with a plastic device that measured the amount of air I could inhale. I struggled to get past 200 while the device measured up to 4000. To help, I used a pillow shaped like a lung to cough, which hurt more than it helped. The therapist also had me walk up and down the hallway while they monitored my heart and oxygen levels using a device that resembled a mind-control gadget more than anything else. They even had to attach it to my head, leaving my butt and balls hanging out with a catheter in place. At that point, I didn't care; strangely, it was building my confidence and making me more comfortable with myself. I managed to make it to the end of the hallway when the nurse asked, "Do you want to keep going, man?"

As I trudged forward, my legs feeling like dead weights, I refused to give up. Slowly but surely, my breathing became less choppy and more steady, a sign that my lungs were growing stronger. As I passed by a large window, the brightness of the snow outside burned my eyes. In the distance, I heard a woman screaming, and I couldn't help but ask,
"What's that noise?"
The nurse's response was solemn. "That's the psych ward. It's a sad place, man. Really sad."

We walked back to my room, where my parents had brought coffee and were waiting for me. We spent the rest of the day together in my room, just talking and enjoying each other's company.

That evening, as I attempted to use the epidural, it suddenly sprayed all over my bed. As it turned out, there had been a hole in it the entire time. The medical team had no choice but to remove it, which, while painful, was not as excruciating as having the chest tubes in. They then replaced my bed, and I was finally able to get some much-needed rest. The following day, during my therapy session, they discovered that the hole had closed up, which led to discussions about taking out the chest tubes. They took me down to the radiology department for a CT scan, which left a burn on my chest. However, the results were impressive as the lung had partially collapsed but had managed to re-inflate. That night, a nurse walked in and informed me that the medical team had cleared me to have my catheter removed and that there was talk of removing my chest tubes the next day.

I exclaimed, "Okay, that's great!" with a forced smile. But the thought of removing the catheter made me feel uneasy. I knew it was going to be painful, and my face twisted in disgust as I asked the nurse, "Is it going to hurt?"
She assured me that it would only sting a little, but it ended up hurting like hell when she pulled the catheter out after counting to two. I tried my best not to scream out loud, but the pain was excruciating.
The nurse reminded me that I had to pee by myself now, or else I would have to go through the catheterization process again. I nodded, trying to hide my discomfort, and she instructed me not to flush after I peed so she could check it. I made my way to the bathroom, but my bladder didn't cooperate at first. I waited anxiously for a few minutes until finally, a stream of urine came out.
"Okay, I peed," I called out, feeling a strange mix of relief and embarrassment, like a child showing off their potty-training skills to their parents.

As I lay on my hospital bed, my mind was a jumble of thoughts and emotions. The pain in my chest was intense, a constant burning sensation that made it hard to focus on anything else. I chuckled a little bit, trying to distract myself from the pain. But even that small movement sent a sharp, searing pain through my body. I had to turn my mind to something else.

Just then, the nurse walked in, her friendly smile and reassuring presence a welcome relief from the pain. I stood up slowly, wincing as I did so, and showed her what I had done in the bathroom. I washed my hands and gave her a high-five, grateful for her kindness and patience.

As we made our way back to my bed, I couldn't help but notice how much pain I was in. My parents came in with pizza a little while later, and my brother and his family showed up shortly after. I was glad to see them, but I didn't enjoy having so many people around me, especially with little kids. They left shortly thereafter, and I was left alone with my pain once again.

Then the nurse came in with some news. "Okay, Mr. Combs. You have been cleared for your chest tubes to be removed, so I'm gonna have you lay on your side."

I felt a wave of fear and anticipation wash over me. I knew this was going to hurt, possibly even worse than the first time. But I also knew that it was necessary to continue my recovery. So I lay on my side and braced myself for the worst.

The nurse began to clip the staples to the back and then the front of the chest tube. She grabbed the back one and said, "Okay. Grunt." I took a deep breath and grunted as she pulled, feeling the tube slowly slide out. It scraped and stung, and my eyes began to swim with tears. The pain was intense.

"Okay, you did well. Now for the last one," she said, grabbing the front. "Grunt." I grunted again, feeling the tube come out with the same scraping, stinging sensation as before. My heart was pounding, and cold perspiration formed on my forehead.

"Okay, today it says you're scheduled for a shower. When you get home, do not take a bath. Those holes in your chest have to be healed from the inside out."

As soon as the nurse mentioned the holes in my chest, a wave of nausea hit me like a ton of bricks. I remembered how I had stopped taking baths when I was 13, and the idea of soaking in a tub while my chest wounds bubbled and filled with water made me feel even worse. I decided to call it a night and try to sleep off the feeling.

The next morning, however, there was no escaping the reality of the situation. I had to take a shower and clean out the wounds. I went through my usual routine of shaving and washing my hair, trying to ignore the gnawing feeling in my stomach. When I stepped into the warm water, it immediately relaxed my tense body, and the humidity filled my lungs, making them feel a little better.

After I got out of the shower, I felt a lot better than I had in days. The experience seemed to clear my mind, and I felt more alert and focused. I had been in a drug-induced fog for the past four days, and pain had been my constant companion. But now, as I got dressed, I felt like I was starting to turn a corner.

Just then, a nurse came into the room with a smile on her face. "Good news," she said. "Your last CT scan and X-ray came back, and they have cleared you to go home." The relief flooded over me, and I couldn't help but smile. It was finally over, and I could start the long road to recovery.

As the nurse told me the news of my release, I couldn't help but feel elated with happiness. "Awesome!" I exclaimed, but the joy was quickly overshadowed by the pain I was still experiencing. I started to question whether it was wise to go home so soon, as most people spend at least a week or two weeks recovering from a thoracotomy. Despite my doubts, I told my parents and they were just as thrilled as I was. I was ready to go home, and so was my family.

A little while later, the nurse returned for my release and I sat at the foot of my bed, slowly putting my clothes back on. As I tried to hold back a cough, I realized I physically couldn't cough and started to hack instead. The pain in my chest and back pulsated with each hack. Then, when I brought up what I thought was phlegm, I saw that it was a jelly-like substance that had been blood at one point. I just sat there in shock and looked up at the nurse. "Is that normal?" I asked, my voice barely above a whisper.

She examined the substance and said, "Yes, that's actually a good sign. You have to realize that they took out a little bit of your lung-"

I was shocked and taken aback, "What do you mean they cut out a part of my lung?" I asked incredulously. I had no idea that the mass was so large that they had to take out a section of my lung. I had assumed that they only removed the gunk and nothing else. My mind was racing with questions and concerns, but I tried to push them aside and focus on getting ready to go home.

I slowly got dressed, feeling the pain in my chest and back with every movement. As I was getting ready, they brought in a wheelchair to take me to the exit. I stood up, but my legs were still weak and shaky from being in bed for so long. I sat down in the chair with my bags and supplies and they began to push me towards the elevator. As we made our way through the hospital, I realized how little I knew about the place. I had only been in one small section and had no idea of the vastness of the hospital.

As we approached the elevator, a thought came to me. Maybe life was like this. We spend our entire lives in our small worlds, only to be brought out into a larger world, and then even larger still. The sedation and pain made me feel philosophical, and I was amazed at how little I knew about the world around me.

Finally, we arrived at the doors to the outside, and my parents were waiting in the car. They helped me into the car, and we began the journey home.

During the ride back home, I reclined my chair and tuned into PewDiePie on YouTube, but my attempts at laughter were thwarted by the pain. So I switched to a documentary on Malcolm in the Middle. Upon arriving home, I was relieved to see the familiar mint-green house. There was still a thick layer of snow on the ground, and without shoes, my mom retrieved my cowboy boots, complete with metal chains and silver plating. I always thought I looked cool in those boots, and I still do. As I maneuvered through the snow, arching my back, I heard my neighbor from across the street yell out, "Looking good, Kyle!"

As we made our way up to the front porch, Sammy, our American Bulldog, greeted me with her tail wagging so hard that I was afraid it would hit me on the side. I sat down on the couch in the living room, but it was uncomfortable compared to my bed upstairs. Walking upstairs was out of the question due to my breathing difficulties. So, I lay down and fell asleep. When I woke up, my mom gave me my prescription of painkillers and muscle relaxers. I took them and dozed off again. I woke up at three in the morning and turned on the TV, but nothing was amusing. As time passed, I started feeling depressed because none of my friends visited me during my hospital stay, and I felt lonely. I thought to myself that I should have died in the hospital. It was then that I realized that family is the only one who will always be there for you.

A few days later, my brother and his family came over to visit and share their pregnancy news. We started brainstorming names for the baby, and I suggested the name Kuklinski for a boy. It was not entirely funny, but I found it amusing because I was on Percocet, and it was the last name of a notorious hitman for the mob in the '80s.

The name they settled on is Rostin, and he is currently three years old. He is such a handful, but according to my parents, he acts just like how I used to act at his age, his uncle. My other nephew Keaton is seven, and even though he is still little, he has a great sense of humor. Sometimes we don't get along because he acts just like his dad, but he's still my best friend.

I quickly realized my mistake as I tried to stifle a laugh, but my chest began to do its little up-down shuffle that it does when I find something funny. Tears streamed down my face and before I knew it, I was sobbing from the pain. The next day, my parents moved my bed to the spare bedroom downstairs where I could be alone. It became my refuge from everyone else. I spent my days watching Star Trek and Bob Ross videos while doing my breathing exercises. It took some time, but I finally reached 500 on the little plate, which was a big improvement from just a few days prior. Over time, I turned the spare bedroom into my activity center, doing puzzles and playing video games on my computer. Eventually, I hit a major milestone, reaching 1000, which meant I was finally taking at least a liter of air per breath. One day, I heard a knock on the door, and when I opened it, there stood a man and a woman who I recognized from years ago when a friend's grandfather had lung cancer. They had brought me a card and a coupon book for a local restaurant. It really surprised me and made me realize that my friends cared about me too, not just my family. I thanked them from the bottom of my heart.

A week later, I have an appointment with my family doctor. As he walks in, he exclaims, "Look who it is! The mystery man himself!"
I let out a small laugh and ask, "Mystery man?"
He replies, "Yes, mystery man. They still can't figure out what's causing your symptoms. It's not cancer, it's not pneumonia. We need to take another look at your chest."
He sends me back across the hall and at this point, I stop taking Percocet to avoid getting addicted. After the x-ray, the doctor returns with bad news.
"That doesn't look good," he says, causing my stomach to drop.
"What? What do you mean?" I ask anxiously.
"It looks like it's starting again on top of the lung," he responds with a thoughtful expression.
I start to panic, but he interrupts my thoughts.
"Let's not jump to conclusions. Do you feel okay?"
"Yeah, just a little unsteady from not taking the Percocet. I don't want to get addicted again," I explain.
He asks, "Do you have them on you?"

I nod and show him the pills. He instructs me to take one and meet him back in the office in twenty minutes. As I walk back to the radiology department, I hope that this new scan will provide some answers.

As he looked at the x-ray, he commented, "Ah, that slant made it appear worse than it is." He pointed at the top of my lung, where there was a clear indentation, reminiscent of the pleurisy I had before. "I'll send these x-rays over to the surgeon in Kettering for a second opinion, because I don't know what the hell that is," he continued. My mom took a week off work to stay with me, and the following days were nerve-wracking as we waited for answers. Eventually, the surgeon called me in for an appointment on Friday. We made our way back to Kettering, and after a brief wait, we were ushered into a small room. The doctor walked in and said, "Hello, Mr. Combs, I have some good news. The spot above your lung is common and it's what happens when we do these kinds of surgeries. It's air, and the clouding is blood. The air will eventually dissipate on its own."
I asked, "And what's the bad news?"
He replied, "What? There is no bad news. In the worst-case scenario, we might have to perform a thoracentesis to get the air out, but that is unlikely."

"Okay," I replied with a hint of unease. The doctor stood up and shook my hand, assuring me, "You'll be fine. Your recent CT scan from today will be looked at. If you don't hear from us, then this concludes our meetings, hopefully for good."
As it turned out, we never heard from them again. With time, my breathing improved and grew stronger. Though I was still on medical leave, I visited work occasionally to catch up on things and see everyone.
My manager asked, "When do you plan on coming back?"
"I'm not sure. They still have me on medical leave," I responded.
"Well, we had to transfer you," he said.
"Where?" I asked.
"We're not sure yet, but you're definitely not going to be in the freezer section anymore," he chuckled.
After that conversation, we left and I returned home.

During that period, I received assistance from numerous doctors and surgeons, and I am grateful for all their efforts, except for Dr. S. You see, as I mentioned earlier, I was not afraid to speak out about Dr. S, but now I am hesitant because I do not want to face a defamation lawsuit.

Realizing that you care more for people who don't reciprocate is incredibly frustrating. After all these years of being close to people from pre-school to high school, it's disappointing to see that they couldn't even be bothered to check in on me. It's a lesson that when we invest so much time in others, we need to stop and consider if they would do the same for us, which most won't. Changing can mean losing friends, losing interest in jobs or activities, but that's part of life. Not everyone will stay in our lives forever, and if we can't accept that, we'll never be able to change. Comfort zones can hold us back, but breaking free from them can lead to extraordinary things. Don't doubt yourself or explain yourself to others, focus on setting positive changes in motion. Surround yourself with supportive people who uplift you and block out negativity, even if it comes from family. Toxicity doesn't discriminate, and negativity won't help you succeed. So make some changes and strive towards a positive and fulfilling life.

Back in the Aisles:
My Second Act at Walmart

My confidence was soaring. Nothing seemed to hold me back anymore. Most people would have given up after enduring the pain and suffering I went through, but not me. I had started attending church again with a few of my friends and life was finally getting back on track. It was a chilly February day, and I had just celebrated my 20th birthday. I was now able to breathe better and felt well enough to drive myself around town again. I had my final appointment with the lung doctor. This time, I wasn't the quiet, sickly kid anymore. I sat with my dad as they conducted the breathing test on me, and the results were exceptional. As the doctor walked in and sat down, he asked me what the other doctors had said, and I watched him jot down notes.
"Looks like there was an issue with your last CT scan," he said, turning to me.
I exchanged a perplexed look with my dad. "What do you mean?" I asked.

"Well, I'm already cleared of that," I explained. "I spoke with the surgeon and he did another chest tube procedure to fix it."
The doctor nodded. "Oh, okay. So he knows."
"Yes, he said it reduced," I replied confidently.
The doctor hesitated. "Actually, it looks like it got worse," he said, watching for my reaction.
I asked for the date he was referring to and confirmed that I had already had another CT scan since then and was cleared by the doctors at Kettering. The doctor then requested to see the CT scan, but I refused, trusting the professionals who had already given me the all-clear.
"Alright then, I guess that concludes our appointment," he said, standing up. As I walked past him, he added, "If you have any more issues, feel free to send over the x-rays and we'll figure it out."
"Sure, we will." I simply replied.

Dear reader, this is what we call a fear-mongering physician. Another word for such a doctor is "alarmist" - someone who deliberately causes fear or panic in their patients. I believe that Dr. S was intentionally trying to keep me scared and anxious so that I would keep coming back to him. If he ever comes across this book (and I'm sure he'll know it's about him), I might even send him a signed copy. Dr. S, you are one of the most thoughtless doctors I have ever encountered, and you are a disgrace to anyone who holds that title. While you may have helped me to some extent, your lack of skill prevented you from completing my surgery.

We left the doctor's office, and he did what he was supposed to do - help me. I had found someone who could assist me with any future issues. The following week, I had increased the capacity of my breathing machine to three thousand, inching closer to my goal of four thousand. Singing became my favorite exercise as it helped me strengthen my lungs. However, my back had become sore, and my left arm had weakened. Despite my lungs being able to hold a lot of air, I still experienced intermittent gasping. Nevertheless, I persisted with my exercises. As February drew to a close, I was eager to return to work and start earning money, mostly to pay off the overwhelming hospital bills that burdened me.

I made another appointment with my family doctor, but as I sat in my car for ten minutes before going in, I questioned myself, "Is this what I really want?" Despite the doubts, I went in determined to show them that I was in the best health possible. After signing in, I was called back by the nurse who recorded my weight - I had gained ten pounds, bringing me to 134 lbs. Although I still had a way to go from my previous weight of 155 lbs, it was a fair improvement. The doctor came in shortly after and greeted me with enthusiasm, "Kyle! How's my mystery-man doing?"
"I'm feeling a lot better now that I can breathe without pain," I replied.
"That's great news! So, what can I help you with today?"
"I'm ready to get back to work now. I think three months off is enough," I said with a smile.
"Okay, but they don't have you back in the freezers still, do they?"

When I returned the following week with all my paperwork, I had to resubmit a transfer request for the lawn and garden section. Fortunately, they didn't have me back in the freezers. The week after, I started back and was elated to be working again. I had so much optimism about the future. They even scheduled me as a caterer for the plant, where every morning I came in and watered and pruned the plants. It was a great job at first, but as the days progressed, I found the lifting and the dampness, on top of the cold, was affecting my breathing. The surgery I had undergone made my left arm very weak, and the epidural they gave me made my entire back ache consistently. But what really bothered me was my managers. It wasn't what they said, it was what they wouldn't say. So, after a year of many hours devoted to the company, I turned in my vest.

The managers appeared to treat me with a certain level of hostility, likely due to my ongoing health issues. While they weren't outright disrespectful, I sensed a difference in their attitudes towards me, especially with the new managers who took over during my absence. Despite my love for the job, the mental and physical strains of returning became overwhelming, and I ultimately had to leave. Years later, during the COVID pandemic, I attempted to return, but the company culture and atmosphere had drastically changed. Many of my former coworkers had moved on, and the company itself was not the same. Unfortunately, my return was short-lived due to these changes.

I fell back into a state of depression, feeling like I had no other choice but to come to a conclusion. Despite the stress of medical bills with FINAL NOTICE stamped across them, I still put on a facade of happiness in front of my family. But when it was just me and the man in the mirror, it was raining on the inside and I spent days on end in bed. The thought of suicide crept into my mind more and more frequently. Desperate for a change, I began searching for a new job, even if it meant settling for an office job. I applied for a position at a factory that made incense, but despite hitting it off with the owner during the interview, I received an email declining my application due to my health issues. It broke my heart, and little things like this denial only added to my downward spiral. I locked myself away in my room again, not coming out for a week.

During that time, my uncle came over and we were all downstairs discussing my job situation. As an owner of a construction business, he asked why I hadn't found a job yet. I explained that my back and chest were still causing me issues.

"So?" he interrupted. "Let me tell you a little story. When I was 23, I fell from a board about 20 feet up in the air and landed on my back. My heart stopped, and I was dead until they shocked me back to life in the ambulance. The doctors and nurses told me I would never work again and suggested disability, but I had a family to support. So, I signed myself out and went back to work that Thursday."

I was speechless, but his words stayed with me. Even though bad things had happened to me, I couldn't let them define my future. At 20 years old, I had my whole life ahead of me, and I wasn't going to let the past hinder my self-growth. Life might not be easy or fair, but it's up to us whether we let it push us around.

Up in Smoke:
My Journey to Discovering the Cause of My Lung Issues

I was done being the "Mystery Man" and having unanswered questions. So I scoured the internet for information on smoking and pleurisy. After reading numerous medical journals, I finally arrived at a single diagnosis: Wet-lung. This condition is caused by bacteria-related fluid from vaping products, which can cause the lungs to fill with water. Looking back, I remembered feeling a bubbling sensation in my lungs before I quit vaping. What disturbed me most was the lack of discussion on this condition. Although there were several cases across America and the world, every article I found made it seem like a rarity. But I knew from my experience that wet-lung was the only plausible explanation for my condition, and I paid for it dearly.

I approached my final x-ray armed with my own research and findings. As I entered the doctor's office, I presented my stack of papers and confidently stated my case.
"After extensive research, I believe my condition is caused by wet-lung, a result of vaping. These reports support my theory and reveal a trend of misdiagnoses and pleurisy related to this condition."
The doctor carefully reviewed my papers and acknowledged my self-diagnosis.
"Wow, you may have hit the nail on the head. Let's take a final look at those lungs and send these findings to some colleagues for further review."
Feeling empowered, I bravely underwent my final x-ray and was relieved to see improvement in my lungs. As I left the doctor's office, I shed my former identity as the mystery man and embraced my new moniker: Iron Lung, the Worry Wart.

Final Statement.

Through this personal account, I aim to provide insights into the correlation between lung issues and vaping. I hope that by sharing my experience, readers can learn something new. For those who seek further information, there is a growing body of research that suggests vaping can cause lung damage and illness.

There has been growing concern and controversy over the correlation between lung issues and vaping. While vaping has been promoted as a safer alternative to smoking, recent studies and reports have raised alarms about potential health risks associated with vaping, particularly related to lung health.

One of the major health concerns related to vaping is the development of what is known as "wet-lung," a condition in which a person's lungs fill with fluid. This condition is particularly associated with vaping due to the chemicals present in e-cigarettes and vaping products, which can cause severe inflammation in the lungs, leading to difficulty breathing, chest pains, and coughing. In some severe cases, wet-lung can lead to hospitalization and even death.

The vapor from e-cigarettes and vaping products contains a variety of chemicals, including nicotine, formaldehyde, and other harmful compounds. These chemicals can cause inflammation in the lungs, leading to respiratory distress and other lung issues. Studies have shown that vaping can lead to a higher incidence of respiratory problems, such as bronchitis and pneumonia, particularly in people who have underlying health conditions like asthma.

In addition to the chemicals present in e-cigarettes, the way in which people use these products may also contribute to lung issues. Many people use e-cigarettes and vaping products by inhaling deeply and holding the vapor in their lungs for longer periods of time, which can lead to increased exposure to harmful chemicals.

Another issue related to vaping and lung health is the use of flavorings in e-cigarettes and vaping products. While many people enjoy the variety of flavors available, the chemicals used to create these flavors can be harmful when inhaled. Some studies have suggested that flavorings in e-cigarettes can cause inflammation in the lungs and lead to the development of respiratory problems.

Overall, the correlation between lung issues and vaping is a complex issue that requires further research and investigation. While vaping has been marketed as a safer alternative to smoking, recent studies and reports suggest that there are potential health risks associated with the use of these products. As such, it is important for people to be aware of the potential risks associated with vaping and to make informed decisions about their health.

As of the current year, 2023, this book was originally written in 2019 and it was given the title "Iron-Lung the Worry-Wart". Since then, I have written three other books, namely "Made in America: Why Domestic Manufacturing is Vital for Our Future", "The West Coast Crisis: Drugs, Homelessness, and Despair in Modern America", and "Mastering Your Anger: Practical Strategies for Managing Your Emotions and Improving Your Life". All of these books can be found on Amazon. I hope that you enjoyed reading this personal account and thank you for taking the time to do so.